GOD
SEEKER

I0112292

GOD
SEEKER

"I have found David…
a man seeking My heart"

God, Acts 13:22, ELT

ELMER TOWNS

© Copyright 2021–Elmer L. Towns

All rights reserved. This book is protected by the copyright laws of the United States of America. This book may not be copied or reprinted for commercial gain or profit. The use of short quotations or occasional page copying for personal or group study is permitted and encouraged. Permission will be granted upon request. Unless otherwise identified, Scripture quotations are taken from the NEW AMERICAN STANDARD BIBLE., Copyright©1960,1962,1963,1968,1971,1972, 1973,1975,1977 by The Lockman Foundation. Used by permission. Scripture quotations marked NKJV are taken from the New King James Version. Copyright © 1982 by Thomas Nelson, Inc. Used by permission. All rights reserved. Scripture quotations marked ESV are taken from The Holy Bible, English Standard Version. (ESV.), copyright © 2001 by Crossway, a publishing ministry of Good News Publishers. Used by permission. All rights reserved.

All emphasis within Scripture quotations is the author's own. Please note that Destiny Image's publishing style capitalizes certain pronouns in Scripture that refer to the Father, Son, and Holy Spirit, and may differ from some publishers' styles.

DESTINY IMAGE® PUBLISHERS, INC.
P.O. Box 310, Shippensburg, PA 17257-0310
"Promoting Inspired Lives."

This book and all other Destiny Image and Destiny Image Fiction books are available at Christian bookstores and distributors worldwide.

Cover design by Eileen Rockwell

For more information on foreign distributors, call 717-532-3040.

Reach us on the Internet: www.destinyimage.com.

ISBN 13 TP: 978-0-7684-6288-3

ISBN 13 eBook: 978-0-7684-6289-0

For Worldwide Distribution.

1 2 3 4 5 6 7 8 / 25 24 23 22 21

CONTENTS

Introduction 11

PART ONE

Chapter 1   David—Faithful as a Young Shepherd 17

Chapter 2   David—Faithfully Fights Evil 29

Chapter 3   David—Faithfully Writing Psalms To God 37

Chapter 4   David—Faithful to God's Calling 47

Chapter 5   David—Faithful as a New King 57

Chapter 6   David—Faithful to Repent After Terrible Sin 71

Chapter 7   David—Faithful at the End 85

Afterthought 97

PART TWO

Week One   David—
Faithful as a Shepherd 107

Day 1   Go...Find My King 108

Day 2   Where Was David When He Was Found? 110

Day 3   Qualifications 112

Day 4   David—the Eighth Son 114

Day 5   God's Eyes 116

Day 6   The Spirit Moves 118

Day 7   David—the Best 120

Week Two   David—
             Faithfully Fights Evil 123

Day 8   Focus 124

Day 9   Faithful to Small Responsibilities 126

Day 10   Wear Your Own Armor 128

Day 11   The Inner You 130

Day 12   Victory Before the Battle 132

Day 13   Face Your Problems 134

Day 14   Finish the Job 136

Week Three   David—
             Faithfully Writing Psalms to God 139

Day 15   David Hungered After God 140

Day 16   Pray the Psalms 142

Day 17   Psalms of Deep Feelings 144

Day 18   The Future 146

Day 19   Prayer for Wisdom 148

Day 20   Psalms When You Sin 150

Day 21   Psalms of Worship 152

Week Four   David—
               Faithfully to God's Calling 155

Day 22   Jealousy Began It All. 156

Day 23   David the Fugitive. 158

Day 24   How Long in the Wilderness .160

Day 25   The Patience of Faith 162

Day 26   More Patience of Faith. 164

Day 27   What to Do When God Does Not Answer 166

Day 28   God Replaced Saul with David 168

Week Five   David—
               Faithfully as a New King 171

Day 29   Waiting to Move Up. 172

Day 30   Only Half the Kingdom 174

Day 31   Unity at Last. 176

Day 32   Committed to Doing Right 178

Day 33   Dreams of Jerusalem. 180

Day 34   New Attack. 182

Day 35   Right Thing...Wrong Way 184

Week Six   David—
               Faithfully to be Restored After Terrible Sin 187

Day 36   David's Sin. 188

Day 37   Thou Art the Man 190

Day 38   God's Mercy 192

Day 39   David Prayed and Fasted 194

Day 40   What Repentance Looks Like 196

Day 41   Repentance Leads to Victory 198

Day 42   David's Thanks for Peace 200

Week Seven David—
            Faithful Beyond His Physical Life 203

Day 43   Who Will Take David's Place 204

Day 44   That Which Cost Me Nothing 206

Day 45   God-Seeking 208

Day 46   David Thinks About the Future 210

Day 47   Your Body a Temple 212

Day 48   David's Example 214

Day 49   Be a God-Seeker 216

Part Three

Lesson Intro (**A Key**) David Found Faithfulness in God's Heart . . 220

Lesson Intro (**Q**) David Found Faithfulness in God's Heart 224

Lesson 1:   (**A Key**) David—
              Faithful as a Young Shepherd 228

Lesson 1:   (**Q**) David—
              Faithful as a Young Shepherd 232

Lesson 2:   (**A Key**) David—
              Faithfully Fights Evil 236

Lesson 2:   (Q) David—
             Faithfully Fights Evil 239

Lesson 3:   (A Key) David—
             Faithfully Writing Psalms to God 242

Lesson 3:   (Q) David—
             Faithfully Writing Psalms to God 247

Lesson 4:   (A Key) David—
             Faithful to God's Calling. 252

Lesson 4:   (Q) David—Faithful to God's Calling. 255

Lesson 5:   (A Key) David—
             Faithful as a New King. 259

Lesson 5:   (Q) David—
             Faithful as a New King. 263

Lesson 6:   (A Key) David—
             Faithful to Be Restored After Terrible Sin 267

Lesson 6:   (Q) David—
             Faithful to Be Restored After Terrible Sin 272

Lesson 7:   (A Key) David—
             Faithful Beyond His Physical Life. 276

Lesson 7:   (Q) David—
             Faithful Beyond His Physical Life. 280

PART FOUR

PowerPoint Guide. 285

PART FIVE

Additional Resources 297

Introduction

GOD-SEEKER

"I have found David—a man seeking My heart."

Acts 13:22, ELT

WHAT is a *God-seeker*? It is a man or woman who gives 100% of their heart, soul, and energy to seek the Lord. David was a *God-seeker*, and he used the word *seek* to describe his search for God.

God said to David, "Seek ye My face," then David responded, "Thy face, Lord I will seek" (Psalm 27:8). And what is seeking God's face? It is worship—giving the total response of your heart to God in praising Him, magnifying Him, and adoring Him. How did David worship" One thing have I desired of the LORD, that will I seek after, that I may dwell in the house of the LORD all the days of my life, to behold the beauty of the LORD" (Psalm 27:4-5).

And what is seeking or searching? First, God-seekers are seen by three distinctly different, but also three total dedicated efforts of your time...talent ... and totally commitment of your mind, emotions, and physical energy to find a treasure. The treasure David sought was the presence of God.

Second, your search must focus on every conceivable place where God could be found., You may seek God in many books—written by great Christian authors, but you will find God in one book, seek Him in His Word. But, you also seek Him with your mind and mouth—you seek God in prayer. You tell God why you search for Him and how much He means to you. You seek God with your heart because you love Him.

But there is a third aspect of seeking—it has to do with why you want to find. If you search for $10 it is because you need that money. If you search for your lost child on a playground, it is because you are terrified what might happen to your little one. But mostly for love, you search because you love him/her. So when you search for God, you seek with your whole heart, soul, and body But, God is not lost! He wants to be found, He wants you to give your whole life searching for Him.

- You search for oneness with your lost love—that is how God responds.

- You search for security, knowing you are not in danger—that is what God gives.

- You search for peace to your troubled mind—God enjoys your new found confidence.

- You search for relief from distress and fear—God wants to enter your new found calmness.

- You search for happiness—God want you to rejoice and He is like the shepherd who found his one lost sheep. "He will joyfully carry it home on his shoulders...rejoice with me ... and there is joy in heaven" (Luke 15:5, 7, NLT).

What will you get reading *God-seeker*? Just as David found the heart of God (Acts 13:22), so you can find the heart of God. When you look into God's heart, you will not see an empty organ...nor will you see muscles pumping energy at to the body. NO! when you find the heart of God, you will discover enteral life.

You will find love in God's heart. He loves every person born into His world (John 3:16). And the Father so loved them that He sacrificed His Son Jesus to die for their sins, so they don't have to die and be punished in hell. Isn't love sacrificing? Look at a mother going through pain, sacrificing for the birth of her child. Look at a mother sacrificing her time to touch and protect her child. Look at a mother sacrificing her money and physical energy for her child because of love.

When you seek the heart of God, you will find His love, just as David first found love for God, then love for others, and third, love for the mission God gave him.

Another thing David found in the heart of God—holiness. The angels around God's throne crying, "holy, holy, holy" (Isaiah 6:3; Revelation 4:8). When you find God's holiness, you learn that you are a corrupt sinner—as far from holiness as any lost person. But Jesus died to forgive your sins and in His sacrifice He made us holy and righteous before God. We are not holy in ourselves, No! "God made Christ who never sinned to be the offering for our sins, so that we could be made right (holy) with God" (2 Corinthians 5:21, NLT).

David learned holiness and lived by that guiding star. That does not mean David never sinned—for there are illustrations in Scriptures of David's terrible sins—but it means David sought to please God in all he did, and as a result, "David found favor with God" (Acts 7:46). So when David was seeking God, what did he find? *Favor*—David was one of God's favorites.

But David also found worship as he was seeking God. Some people don't know what to say when they approach God, what to do, nor do they know how to act. As a God-seeker, David learned to worship. If you want to worship the Lord effectively become a God-seeker like David.

So why read or devour this short book? It will educate you about David's life—but more than that. This book will examine the way God led David and tell you how God will lead you—but more. This book will explain the secret of David's victory over Goliath, and the Philistines, and all his enemies who attack him—but more. This book will explore some of David's Psalms as he became a *God-seeker*—but more. This book is written to guide you on an exciting journey so you feel what David felt when he felt the heart of God. This book wants to lead you to seek God as David was a *God-seeker*, so you discover what David discovered; so you experience the heart of God...so you experience Him with all your mind...your love...your decision-making choices...and your devotion.

This book invites you to be a *God-seeker*.

Sincerely yours in Christ,

Elmer Towns

Written in my 89th year, having followed Christ since I was 17 years old

PART ONE

GOD SEEKER

Chapter 1

DAVID – FAITHFUL AS A YOUNG SHEPHERD

D AVID'S name in Hebrew means *beloved*. It is a name given to him at birth. About the time David was circumcised, the father announced, "his name is David." The boy was beloved by his parents and also by God.

David is a personal name prized and revered by Jewish people. As a result no baby boy was given the name David in the years following David's reign as king. Oh there may have been some boys named David here and there, but none to catch our attention like king David, son of Jesse from Bethlehem.

DAVID—NEW THINGS

David was the youngest of eight children. Those who examined numerology in the Bible note that number seven stands for completion, as seven days in a week or seven notes in the musical scale. But the number eight stands for *new beginnings*, or *new life*. So, David the eighth child of Jesse brought new spiritual life to God's people, and he also brought a new victories over Israel's enemies, and a new way of looking at the future.

DAVID'S HERITAGE

When studying David's past you cannot forget that Ruth the Moabite was his great grandmother. She was a foreigner who chose to follow Jehovah and came to live in Bethlehem with her mother-in-law Naomi.

The fact that foreign blood (non-Jewish) flowed in David's veins cannot be over looked. Examine carefully the record and you will not find any Jewish lineage or heritage attached to David's mother. Some scholars have suggested that David not only had the blood of Ruth the Moabite running through his veins, some even think that perhaps David's mother was a Moabitess. When David was running from Saul, he put both his father and mother under the protection of the king of Moab (1 Samuel 22:3-4). Because his parents were accepted into Moabite culture, some believe it is because his mother's physical identification with the Moabites.

When we first see David, he is a shepherd looking after sheep. But beyond that he became a musician, a solider, a king, a poet, and through his godly life, he was an influencer for generations to come.

Remember David was born in Bethlehem, the same city were Jesus would later be born. Throughout David's years when chased by Saul, he had a love and infinity for Bethlehem.

Is David the greatest of all Old Testament heroes? Adam began it all...Noah saved the human race through the flood...Abraham was father of the Jewish people...Moses led God's people out of bondage from Egypt, but most of all Moses received the Ten Commandments on top of Mount Sinai. How could David be greater than those extraordinary heroes of faith?

David was important enough to the LORD that His Son Jesus was given the title, *Son of David*! God's city is called *City of David*! Even God described David as "a man after My own heart."

DAVID FOUND FAITHFULNESS IN THE HEART OF GOD

"David...a man seeking God's own heart" (Acts 13:22, ELT)

When David pursed God's heart—what did he find? David found faithfulness. Yes, God is faithful. God's faithfulness is described, "The One who calls you is faithful and He will do what He promises" (1 Thessalonians 5:24, ELT). A faithful God was seeking a man to be king over His people. Because David was a *God-seeker*, God called David to be king of Israel. David became faithful to reflect God's faithfulness.

David also found fellowship in seeking God. As David the shepherd boy was tending sheep, he began writing Psalms at an early age, and found the Lord was his Shepherd who would lead him...protect him though the valley of the shadow of death. So David claimed the promise of Psalm 23, "Thou art with me."

Also David found in God's heart—godly influence...how else could a shepherd boy write such great Psalms? Did he write for himself? No! Did he write for the sheep? No! Did he write for the Hebrews? No! David wrote for God...He wrote about God ...and in the final analysis, David wrote to God. And today we enjoy the Psalm because we experience the God-chaser.

Humans could describe David's strengths in many different ways, but perhaps the best characteristic, David was like God Himself. Didn't God say, "I have found David...a man after My own heart" (Acts 13:22). So, when David searched the heart of God, what did he find? He found the strength of God's faithfulness, and in his search David the God-chaser, became like God—he became faithful to God.

When you read of David's life, think of all the different titles and roles he played. First David was a shepherd...then a musician...next a warrior who killed Goliath...then he was an outcast running from king Saul who was hunting David to kill him. During all this time David was a poet writing some of the greatest Psalms in history. But beyond all of this David was a statesman, a king, and in that role was the spiritual leader of Israel—God's people.

Technically David began his life as a shepherd boy, then after he killed Goliath his popularity grew. "The women sang, 'Saul has slain his thousands, and David his ten thousands'" (1 Samuel 18:7). Quickly he was suspect by king Saul who thought David might take his throne. David became an exile, not living in his hometown of Bethlehem, nor ever in his own nation. He lived among foreign nations. Finally after many years, David became king.

Perhaps one of the most touching incidences in David's solider-exile life was during his war with the Philistines. As a small boy, he had drank from the water well in Bethlehem (2 Samuel 23:15, 1 Chronicles 11:17). Again, he yearned for another drink from that well. His mighty men fought their way into Bethlehem, to bring him water from the well in the city that later would be called by his name, *The City of David*. It was then David poured out the water as a sacrifice to God in gratitude for the bravery of men willing to risk all for him.

DAVID ANOINTED KING

The first time David appears in Scripture, was during an annual feast in Bethlehem. God sent Samuel, the prophet of God, and spiritual leader of the nation to Bethlehem with a task. "Fill your horn with oil, and go; I am sending you to Jesse the Bethlehemite. For I have provided Myself a king among his sons" (1 Samuel 16:1). Samuel took a heifer with him to sacrifice to the Lord in their annual feast. The sacrifice was in the home of Jesse, suggesting he was the leader in the town of Bethlehem, a city earlier made famous by David's grandmother Ruth, who left Moab to come live in Bethlehem.

As Samuel prepared to anoint one of Jesse's sons, he made all seven boys pass before him. But God rejected all seven sons saying, "Do not look at his appearance or at his physical stature, because I have refused him. For the Lord does not see as man sees; for man looks at the outward appearance, but the Lord looks at the heart" (1 Samuel 16:7). As seven passed before Samuel, them, God was saying, "The Lord has not chosen these" (1 Samuel 16:10).

Samuel asked the father, "Are all the young men here?" (1 Samuel 16:11). Jesse answered, "There remains yet the youngest, and there he is, keeping the sheep" (1 Samuel 16:11). When David appeared, what did Samuel see? "He was ruddy (auburn hair), with bright eyes, and good-looking" (1 Samuel 16:12).

When David, the youngest son came into the house, the Lord said to Samuel, "Stand up and anoint him. This is the one I have chosen to be king" (1 Samuel 16:12). So Samuel anointed David and the Spirit of the Lord came upon the boy from that day on Still, David went back to his work of caring for his father's sheep, out in the hills around Bethlehem.

David was not only strong in body, but strong in spirit, a young man who had learned to know the Lord as his shepherd. More than once

David had fought off and killed a lion and a bear attacking his sheep. David was an expert in the use of the sling with which he hurled stones to protect the flock.

He became a good musician, playing his harp. But because David loved God, he wrote hymns/Psalm to praise God, singing to Him on his harp. We still have many of those songs of praise today, called Psalms. One of the most beautiful of them is the Shepherd Palm:

Psalm 23

The Lord is my shepherd;

I shall not want.
He makes me to lie down in green pastures;
He leads me beside the still waters.
He restores my soul;
He leads me in the paths of righteousness
For His name's sake.

Yea, though I walk through the valley of the shadow of death,
I will fear no evil;
For You are with me;
Your rod and Your staff, they comfort me.

You prepare a table before me in the presence of my enemies;
You anoint my head with oil;
My cup runs over.
Surely goodness and mercy shall follow me
All the days of my life;
And I will dwell in the house of the Lord
Forever.

Out in the hills David drew closer and closer to the Lord as the Spirit of God was teaching him to be faithful to God in every way. But in the royal palace things were not going so well with king Saul. The Spirit of the Lord had withdrawn from him, and he was becoming moody and unhappy. Sometimes he behaved completely like a madman. His servants were afraid of him. After a while they discovered that when someone quietly played the harp, Saul's bad mood soon became better.

One of the servants remembered that he had seen a young man—the son of Jesse—who not only was a clever player of the harp, but also an expert with the weapons of war.

That young man, David, was brought to Saul.

David's beautiful and soothing harp music made Saul much calmer. David returned again to Bethlehem to be his father's shepherd as he had been before. No one knew that this young man had been anointed to become king in Saul's place.

DAVID DREAMS OF JERUSALEM

Many think of David as a young boy watching his sheep, he lead them approximately ten or twelve miles from Bethlehem to the bottom of a valley where he would look up to see the majestic city of Jerusalem with its high surrounding walls. The Pool of Siloam was at the bottom of the valley looking up to Jerusalem. Next to it was a cave and a tunnel or shaft that opened up inside the walls of Jerusalem. This shaft was actually a well. People in Jerusalem would lower their buckets to be filled in the pool.

Today standing outside the Pool of Siloam in the valley one can look up to see the reconstructed Herod's Temple high above on Mount Zion.

Perhaps as a young boy David had brought his sheep to drink in this fountain. Do you think that young David dreamed of one day capturing that city by climbing up that shaft at night to occupy the city? Do you think David dreamed of ruling from that fortification?

The shaft was cut through rock during the days of king Hezekiah. A long rope over sixty feet in length was used to lift buckets of water from the Pool of Siloam to city of Jerusalem. At night those ropes were pulled up into the city so no one could climb up the sixty feet to gain entrance into Jerusalem.

Yet when a 30 year old king David began his assault to capture the city of Jerusalem, Joab, one of his mighty men climbed up the interior wall without a rope. Some people think he wedged himself against both walls to work himself up sixty feet into the city. Others think that many of David's mighty men formed a high human ladder standing on one another to reach to the top. They entered the city at night and captured it (2 Samuel 5:7-9). The city had a reputation of being so impenetrable it could not be captured. They even bragged, "Even the blind and lame can defend the city" (2 Samuel 5:6).

Up until the appearance of king David as the leader of God's people, there had been no one like him in the history of Israel. David could capture the imagination of common people and inspire their emotions to do more for God, and expect more from the Lord they serve. And why was he great? Look at God's reason for choosing David to be His leader of Israel and king of the nation. God "sought for a man after My heart" (Acts 13:22). David was a *God-seeker*.

A heart for God prepared David to be used by God. When Samuel was looking for a candidate to anoint as the next king over God's people, the Lord said to him, "Look not on his countenance, or on the height of his stature...for the LORD seeth not as man seeth for man looks on the outward appearance, but the LORD looketh on the heart" (1 Samuel 16:7).

The Spirit of God directed David's plans, actions, and emotions. "Samuel took the horn of oil and anointed him...and the Spirit of the Lord came on David" (1 Samuel 16:13). When examining David, we see the anointing influence of God by his careful respect for people around him, his reverence for the Lord's presence as seen in his Psalms, his refusal to murder Saul when given the opportunity even though he had God's anointing for the office of king.

The Lord God had David's vision and purpose of life. As you read David's passion for God in his Psalms, remember David wrote/sang his Psalms about God, and for God; but most of all he prayed his Psalms to God.

TEN WAYS TO PREPARE TO BE GOD'S LEADER

1. *Love the work/ministry God has given you.* David was the youngest of eight sons destined to be a shepherd. When the other seven sons were examined by Samuel to be the next king, David was left out. But you do not sense David felt neglected or discriminated against. No...not at all. He not only loved looking after sheep, he learned from them and saw God working in his life as shepherd.

2. To be effective in ministry, you must love the people to whom you minister. Just as sheep are everything to a shepherd, people are your life, your calling, and your ministry. Any lack of love for them could reflect your lack of love for ministry. You must love them as Christ loved you and gave His life for you.

3. *Identify—so your work/ministry becomes you and you become it.* Not only did David love being a shepherd, he was the protector

of his sheep and provider for his sheep. For the rest of David's life he was identified as a shepherd of sheep, even when he actually was king leading God's people (2 Samuel 7:8).

4. So you must identify with the ministry to which God called you. If it is not as good as you want it to be—make it better. Pray for it, sacrifice for it and make it succeed. Even then, it's success is your success. And in the same way, it's failure is your failure.

5. *Presence—locate yourself with your work/ministry.* David the shepherd had to live with sheep, sleep among sheep, and the sheep were his life. When you serve the Lord, the people to whom you minister are more than people to teach, and people to lead. Your people are your life. Then their life become your life.

6. *Represent yourself with your work/ministry.* David was identified as a shepherd for the rest of his life. When you are given a ministry by God or when you are invited to lead a ministry, you become the representative of that ministry. What people think of you is how they will respect and get involved in that ministry.

7. *Protect what God has given you.* Remember how David protected his sheep. When a predator—bear or lion—attacked his sheep, David did not think of his safety or even his comfort. He went after the predator. In the same way you must protect your people's walk with Christ (purity and testimony). You must also protect them from false doctrine or carnal thinking. Just as David the shepherd protected every part of his sheep's life, so you must protect your followers in doctrine, purity, relationships, spiritual growth, and ministry.

8. *Work for the successes and rewards of your work/ministry.* David's success as a shepherd was measured by the health, prosperity, and growth of his flock of sheep. Because your ministry is you,

then its success and failures are yours. Just as you want to be a "victorious Christian" that gives honor to your Lord, so you want your ministry to be just as successful for the glory of God.

9. *Serve faithfully your work or ministry.* When David became a God-seeker, he sought the Lord with all his heart. What did David find in God's heart? He found faithfulness. Why was David so successful in every aspect of his life? When he found God, he found faithfulness. God motivated David to be faithful, and that became his life's passion.

10. *Associate with the success/failures and the rewards/losses of your work/ministry.* When David told others about how his flock was protected, David was explaining his success. And what reward did he receive? All his sheep were accounted for. That made observers recognize David's excellence in his task of shepherding.

11. *Be totally committed to your work/ministry.* When Samuel showed up at Jesse's home to anoint one of his sons to be the next king, David was not present. The older seven sons reported for inspection. Why did David not show up? Did they not think David qualified? Did anyone suggest they had overlooked David? Did even David ignore the invitation? If he did, perhaps it was because David was totally immersed in his task of being a shepherd. Doesn't that suggest your total commitment to ministering for Christ?

12. *Enjoy the rewards of work/ministry, i.e., meals, anointed head, and living in God's house.* When David wrote Psalm 23 he expressed an enjoyable experiences of serving the Lord who was his Shepherd. David described being led personally by the Lord, enjoying green pastures and quiet waters. He describes being protected among the shadows in death's valley. Then David

described overflowing with food, anointed head, and being followed by the sheep dogs of goodness and mercy.

In a real sense, the happiness of ministering to others is the ministry God gives you as you shepherd God's sheep, which are those to whom you minister.

Chapter 2

DAVID—FAITHFULLY FIGHTS EVIL

DAVID AND GOLIATH

1 Samuel 17:1-54

WHILE David watched the flocks of his father, his three older brothers and those fighting with them engaged in a prolonged stalemate of daily skirmishes with the Philistines which failed to decide a clear victor. The Philistines were life-long enemies of God's people. It was customary among the armies of that day to propose the battle be decided by a championship contest. If a representative champion from each army met in a fight to the death to determine ultimate victory.

Among the Philistines was a man of Gath named Goliath. He stood nine feet three inches tall and would have probably weighed 500-600 pounds. Some writers believe Goliath's mammoth size may have been due to a tumor of the pituitary gland, a known cause of giantism today. Though this may have made Goliath a little clumsy, he was nevertheless well able to handle himself in military conflict. He was "a man of war from his youth" (v. 33) and had earned such a reputation as to be the appointed champion of the Philistines (v. 4).

For forty consecutive days, the giant challenged the army of Israel to a championship battle every morning and evening. The army was probably still engaged in some hand-to-hand conflict during this period, but the lack of military progress against the Philistines together with the constant defiance of Goliath discouraged and scared the Israelite army. The nation Israel was fighting for its national existence, and each day it was becoming increasingly less convinced it could or would win.

As the battle continued into its second month, Jesse became increasingly concerned over the fate of his sons in the army. Because there was not the extensive communications media which exists today, Jesse had probably not heard any reliable news about the battle since his sons left to fight with Saul. He sent his youngest son David to travel to the front and take supplies to his older brothers.

David left early the next morning. He arrived just as the army of Israel was launching its morning offensive and, in his youthful enthusiasm, he joined in. He shouted, cheering on his national army and, after leaving the supplies he had brought with the keeper, ran into the army to join them. Quickly he found his brothers and they began exchanging greetings. Then, for the eighty-first time since the battle had begun forty-one days earlier, the booming voice of Goliath echoed again across the Valley of Elah. "I defy the armies of Israel this day; give me a man, that we may fight together" (v. 10).

As David waited to see who would go out to defeat Goliath, he soon realized there was a real problem. The men who moments before had enthusiastically jumped up and run down toward the battlefield were now fearful and visibly shaken at the appearance of Goliath. As David began to ask questions, he learned the king had offered riches, the hand of his daughter in marriage, and a tax-free status to the man who successfully defeated Goliath. He also learned that none of the men in the army were giving serious thought to collecting the reward.

As his older brother Eliab overheard David's conversations with the other men, he became angry and accusingly misjudged David's motives for being at the front. Eliab's pride had been challenged since his kid brother seemed to think Goliath could be beaten. Probably Eliab was expecting David to begin putting pressure on him to take on Goliath. Eliab, like the rest of Saul's army, did not trust in God for the victory. The very size of Goliath was enough to discourage him from fighting.

In frustration, David responded to Eliab's unwarranted accusations with an expression which has often been repeated, "What have I done now?" (v. 29). David's question was followed by a second which was really more of a statement. "Is there not a cause?" So convicting was the affirmation of David that Eliab was unable to respond. In fact, every time David spoke with confidence that day, he effectively silenced his critics.

The backslidden army of Israel refused to defend the name of its God which had for forty days been blasphemed by the Philistine giant. But David was totally surrendered to the purpose of God and, therefore, willing to fight the necessary battle. As word began spreading through the camp of David's willingness to accept Goliath's challenge, it was not long before David was summoned to appear before King Saul in his tent.

Initially, Saul tried to discourage David from engaging in the battle. David claimed he would be victorious over Goliath because he had been victorious over a bear and lion which had tried to take one of his father's sheep. David attributed his victory over the bear and lion as well as his anticipated victory over Goliath to the Lord. His confident expectation of victory was based on his past experiences of trusting God in a crisis experience. Trusting God in a crisis situation always leads to a greater confidence in God.

When Saul saw he could not dissuade David from fighting Goliath, he agreed but urged him to at least wear his armor. The teenage David stood there as his tall king placed armor on his body. Naturally, the armor designed for the king did not fit the teenager, and David found himself refusing armor for the battle. All he carried into battle that day was his shepherd staff and a sling. While a sling was not the usual sort of weapon one would use in battle, an accurate thrower could throw a stone eighty yards and hit an object as small as a man's head. As David walked down the hill into the valley of Elah that day, he was going to serve God with what was in his hand, separating himself from the unfaithful army of Israel, and standing alone for God against the enemy of God.

PRINCIPLES OF SPIRITUAL VICTORY

1. Total surrender to the purpose of God

2. Future expectations based on past experiences

3. Serve God with what is in your hand

4. Seperate from unfaithful

5. Stand alone

As David passed by the brook, he stooped down and picked up five smooth stones. To this day, the spring floodwaters still deposit thousands of small, round stones in the bed of the brook each year. The question has been asked why David chose five stones if he was trusting God in the battle. Some commentators suggest he chose one for Goliath and one for each of his four brothers. Others argue he choose one stone for each of the five cities of the Philistines. More likely, David simply gathered several stones so as not to be presumptuous as he went out to meet Goliath.

When Goliath realized his challenge was being met by a teenage boy, he began ridiculing David and cursing him. David responded by affirming his confidence that the Lord would give him victory. He appears to have been the only Israelite on the battlefield that still believed "the battle is the Lord's" (v. 47). As David ran toward the Philistine giant, he reached his hand into his bag and took out a stone. Quickly he placed it in his sling and slung it toward Goliath. The stone hit its mark, sinking into the forehead of Goliath. Normally, a man hit by a stone would fall backward, but Goliath fell on his face, indicating he was totally unconscious as a result of the blow. Because David himself did not have a sword, he took the sword of Goliath and used it to sever the giant's head from his body.

With all of the enthusiasm of youth, he then grabbed the head of the giant. Later, David carried it to Jerusalem. Some writers believe David had, even at this early age, planned to someday take Jerusalem and make it his capital. He carried the head of Goliath to show the city—as a warning gesture—Jerusalem's days were numbered.

DAVID: THE CHAMPION OF ISRAEL

1 Samuel 17:55-19:17; Psalm 59

So zealous was David for his first battle trophy that when he appeared before Saul later that day, he was still holding the head of Goliath in his hands. David was not unlike other adolescent youths who wear letter sweaters or other tokens of victory to show off. He was reintroduced to the king, this time not as a minstrel or overly zealous kid, but as a respected and experienced soldier. Even though David was still young, too young to be a man of war, Saul made him a leader in the army and began sending him out to lead soldiers into battle.

TEN STEPS TO FIGHT EVIL

1. *Claim the tools of faith used to win earlier/small victories.* When David went to fight Goliath, he relied on his sling, a rock and his deadly aim. He remembered the lion and bear could have killed or mauled him, but he courageously faced predators with the same courage he faced Goliath. In the same way, you will face the enemies of the world, the flesh and the devil (Ephesians 2:1-2). Therefore, use the tools of Bible memory/quotations, plus prayer and fasting. The tools you successfully use to defeat small obstacles/enemies can work to defeat larger problems. Also, include the ingredients of yieldedness to God, faith, and courage.

2. *Know the source of your attack.* David recognized Goliath represented a greater enemy who was attacking the Lord God Almighty. He ran toward the giant and announced, "He has defied the armies of the living God" (1 Samuel 17:36). When you become a leader, it is not just you the enemy wants to destroy, he also includes the work of God; because stan hates God. So, both you and the work of God need to be defended with the weapons of God.

3. *Depend on spiritual weapons, not secular weapons.* David refused to use Saul's armor, sword, and weapons. He had, "not proved them, and he put them off" (v. 39). Then David choose the weapon he knew best. "He took his staff...five smooth stones... his sling" (v. 40). These were the weapons David used to defeat the lion and the bear. But more importantly, David said, "You come to me with a sword, with a spear, and with a javelin. But I come to you in the name of the Lord of hosts, the God of the armies of Israel" (v. 45).

4. *Be aggressive.* "David hurried...toward...the Philistine" (v. 48). The word *hurried* suggests David aggressively ran toward his enemy. But it even further suggests his unshakeable faith in God. Since God was on his side, why not hurry? Since David had confidence he could win, why not get the battel on ... and get it over with?

5. *Use weapons that have given victory in the past.* David had fought the lion and bear—predators and won. Even in David's battle with predators, he had to be aggressive. He said, "I went after him...smote him...delivered it (sheep) out of his mouth...caught him by his beard, and smote him" (v. 35). David used the same strategy against Goliath that he used against the predators. It might be added, David had the same result.

6. *Faith is your assurance.* David told Goliath, "I come to you in the name of the Lord of hosts, the God of the armies of Israel" (v. 45). And what is faith? It is confidence that God will protect you as He promised, and that God will give victory as He promised.

7. *In battle, remember you are defending God's testimony.* When David went to fight Goliath, he carried the reputation of Israel with him, including the traditions of what God had done in the past through the Judges and other heroes of faith. David said, "... that all the earth may know there is a God in Israel...and this assembly shall know that the Lord does not save with sword and spear; for the battle is the Lord's, and He will give you into our hands." (vv. 46-47). David gave all credit to God before he cast his stone...that is a statement of faith. David knew God would give him victory.

8. *Be resolved for complete victory.* David attacked Goliath reflecting his fierce his determination. "David slung...struck his forehead...the stone sank in...he fell...David ran and stood over

him ... cut off his head" (vv. 49-51). The entire passage reflects David's confidence, but it was not confidence in his ability, or in his weapon; it was confidence in the Lord.

9.   *Encourage others to help*. When the giant fell, the rest of the Philistines began to run away. "The men of Israel...shouted ... pursued the Philistines" (v. 52). It always takes a leader to motivate followers to keep joining in the battle against evil.

10.   *Document your victory*. "David took the head...brought it to Jerusalem" (v. 54). Also, David stood before Saul, "the head... in his hand" (v. 57). Not everyone saw the battle between David and Goliath. They heard reports, but when they saw the head of Goliath, no one could doubt that David had defeated Goliath, or that God had given him the victory.

Chapter 3

DAVID—FAITHFULLY WRITING PSALMS TO GOD

IT is interesting to note that as the Spirit of God came upon David at age 16 when he was anointed king, the very next verse says, "The Spirit of the Lord departed from Saul" (1 Samuel 16::14). This was God's rejection of Saul and His choice of David. Because of Saul's repeated disobedience of God, a troubling or destressing spirit came upon king Saul. Those around the king said let us find a young man who is skillful playing the harp, and when he plays the destressing spirit on Saul will be expelled. The criteria was "A man who can play well" (1 Samuel 16:17).

As they looked around they found the son of Jesse—David. He is described, "who is skillful in playing the harp, a mighty man of valor, a man of war, prudent in speech, and a handsome person; and the Lord is with him" (1 Samuel 16:18). At this place David became more than just a musician playing for the king. The Bible also describes him as Saul's armorbearer. In today's terminology David was an attaché to the chief commanding officer of the nation.

David only visited Saul's encampment on a few occasions to play his harp before the king. It was not David's continuing lifestyle. The Scriptures describe, "But David occasionally went and returned from Saul to feed his father's sheep at Bethlehem" (1 Samuel 17:15). Therefore David's primary task as a teenager was still shepherding his father's sheep.

What do we know about David the shepherd? He usually carried a club and a sling to protect the sheep (1 Samuel 17:40, 43). But he also had a harp to express his heart's emotions.

During those long hours of watching the sheep, how did David spend his time? He practiced slinging a stone until he developed a marvelous accuracy for directly hitting a small target.

But David also spent his time developing his musical ability. This involved three skills, first, playing a musical instrument, second, creating both words and music of Psalms, and third, actually singing them so that David became known as the "singer of Psalms for Israel."

The word for harp was *rubaba*, which was probably a rough one string instrument, but some Bible authorities think it could have two string. The one or two strings would give David the pitch or musical level where he would begin singing his Psalms. But also the harp provided rhythm. David may have strummed the one or two strings to produce a beat or rhythm for his singing.

David composed many of his songs developing his (musical skills) in his causal moments while watching his sheep. These were unpressured time when David also developed his poetical skills (author of words, however, not rhyming words as we use today, but rhyming thoughts). Eventually seventy-three of the Psalms are escribed to David, perhaps he wrote some others that do not have his inscription.

Note that many of David's Psalms were composed with a strong theme of nature as he observed the landscape about him, or the changing weather around him. But David's Psalms were more than observing nature. David gave words and meaning to nature, so that all nature spoke to him; eventually it was nature singing with him, or to him. As a Psalmist, he inscribed what he heard in words then sang it to his sheep. Some were sung to God.

While developing his musical skills and being a shepherd at the same time, David was invited to Saul's palace where he soothed Saul's troubled spirit with his music. It is here that Saul made David his armorbearer (1 Samuel 16:21). Apparently David was extremely effective in his singing because the Bible states, "David would take a harp, and play it with his hand. Then Saul would become refreshed and well, and the distressing spirit would depart from him" (1 Samuel 16:23).

Perhaps David was originally influenced to sing and compose Psalms with the harp by the Sons of the Prophets who were traveling through-out Israel in those days. Even before David is mentioned in Scriptures, the Bible describes God telling Saul that "when you have come there to the city, you will meet a group of prophets coming down from the high place with a stringed instrument, a tambourine, a flute, and a harp before them; and they will be prophesying (1 Samuel 10:5). Perhaps David got some of his motivation from a group like these prophets who were singing and playing.

David is perhaps the most gifted of all the persons in the Old Testament; gifted as a warrior, no one defeated him; gifted as a musician, no one wrote and performed more or better songs/Psalms then him; gifted as a leader, he unified the nation where the northern and southern tribes fought each other, then he was gifted in defending God's people from attacking nations; David conquered all of Israel's enemies, established the monarchy for a time of peace; and David was gifted as statesman, proclaimed peace with many of his neighbors. Perhaps his greatest gift was spiritually lifting the people of God to their highest level of unity... godliness...as he led them to fulfill the promise God had given to their forefathers.

Yet looking deeply into David's role, he was authoritative, yet in his power he was mild. He was fearless against his enemies, yet patiently prayed for God's timing to do things. He had strong impulses, yet took time for people. He had firm faith in God, yet in his unguarded moments we see his weakness and humanity. David was called the *sweet psalmist of Israel* (2 Samuel 23:1). Remember, in the New Testament David was called "a man after God's own heart" (Acts 13:22). David was solider, shepherd, poet, statesman, profit, king, and devoted father.

What could be said of David, he freed his country from its enemies, united the nation into one monarchy, gave them Jerusalem as their capital, established and led the nation in worship of Jehovah and according to many was the ideal leader and the forerunner of the coming Messiah.

David usually composed a song/Psalm to expressing his heart's passion and desire. Yet after he sinned with Bathsheba against Uriah, he lived at least a year without writing any Psalms of confession and repentance.

David didn't write again until Nathan the prophet confronted David with the parable of the rich man taking the lamb from his poor neighbor. David angrily replied, "the wealthy man should pay fourfold to his sin." It is then that Nathan cried out, "Thou art the man" (2 Samuel 12:7, KJV). As a result Psalm 51 is David's confession of guilt and sin. Is it possible that David lived one whole year with sin in his heart and did not deal with it. He had committed adultery, murder, and then did everything he could to cover it up.

Only later when David realized that God accepted his prayers of confession, then he began to write other Psalms of deliverance such as Psalm 32, a hymn of forgiveness, "Blessed is he whose transgression is forgiven, whose sin is covered. Blessed is the man to whom the Lord does not impute iniquity, and in whose spirit there is no deceit" (Psalm 32:1-2). Again David acknowledges his sin, 'I acknowledged my sin to You, and my iniquity I have not hidden. I said, I will confess my transgressions to the Lord, and You forgave the iniquity of my sin'" (Psalm 32:5).

Apparently David could create music and apply it to the situation before him. The genuine emotion of his response to the death of Saul and Jonathan is seen in his song (2 Samuel 1:19-27). Also, his lament over Abner, (2 Samuel 3:23) shows his ability to write and apply music to a current crisis situation.

What do we know about the song writing of David, he was a deeply spiritual man who enjoyed his friendship and communion with God. But just as soon as you say that, you find his high emotional patriotism for the nation. Also, you find his music expressing his deep friendship for others such as Jonathan. But why was David so passionate and devoted to creating Psalms? Because he was an enthusiastic worshiper of Jehovah. His praise to the LORD naturally came out in all his music/Psalms.

David is like other great poets of history who passes through deep experiences...traumatic experiences...life crushing experiences...to response and record one's feelings to tell the outside world what is on the inside. Therefore David's written impression are a reflection of his secretive heart.

But we cannot deny the fact that the source for much of his poetic expression in Psalm was when the Spirit of God that came upon David (1 Samuel 16:13).

MANY TYPES OF PSALMS

Writing made David different from all the young men around him. To be successful, a writer must have insight that others do not possess, then express that truth in a symbolic or demonstrative way. As an illustration, everyone is able to see what is going on around them, but a writer feels their experiences and understands what he sees, and hears. He has the ability to interpret to others what he sees. But his interpretation is more than observation of facts; his words are feelings of action, identification with people and places, so that he expresses in words the cycle of life into action. Yes...what David saw and experienced had meaning to him. And he wrote to communicate life as it occurred.

For much of David's life, he did not have a close friend with whom he could share his experiences. To whom could David tell his feelings when evil men betrayed him, or deceived him, or told lies on him, or tried to kill him. When he could not tell a friend, nor did he have a wife to tell those crushing disappointments—David told these experiences in Psalm.

These Psalms were not a superficial essay about conflicts or aggression, No! They echoed David's heart seeking the Lord. Remember, David is a *God-seeker*.

Unless you had been betrayed as David's enemies lurked against him, you will never understand his Psalms. David poured out his heart to God.

But David was also the optimistic observer who saw the beautiful side of God. David rejoiced in the goodness of God because he had brought his sacrifices to God and felt forgiveness. He could freely and optimistically praise God's forgiveness, because he experienced God's cleansing.

CLASSIFICATIONS OF DAVID'S PSALMS

1. His peaceful early life (8; 19; 29; 23)

2. His persecution by Saul (59; 56; 34; 7; 52; 120; 140; 54; 57; 142; 17; 18)

3. Making David king (27; 133; 101)

4. Bringing up the Ark (68; 24; 132; 15; 78; 6)

5. His first great sin (51; 32)

6. Absalom's rebellion (41; 6; 55; 109; 38; 39; 3; 4; 63; 42; 43; 5; 62; 61; 27)

7. His second great sin (69; 71; 102; 103)

8. The great promise of future kingdom made in 2 Samuel 7 (2:72)

9. Feelings of old age (37)

TEN WAYS TO SEEK GOD'S PRESENCE

1. *Read Psalms to cultivate a hunger for God.* Did David write or sing each Psalm only once? Probably not! David probably repeated the Psalms he wrote many times, especially on occasions when he would benefit from their message. He would need the message of Psalm 27 many times. "One thing I have desired of the Lord, that will I seek: that I may dwell in the house of the Lord all the days of my life, to behold the beauty of the Lord, and to inquire in His temple. For in the time of trouble He shall hide me in His pavilion; in the secret place of His tabernacle He shall hide me; He shall set me high upon a rock" (Psalm 27:4-5).

2. *Pray the Psalms.* Remember, David probably prayed the challenging Psalms when he needed courage, and he prayed the Psalms of consolation when he need comfort. He probably prayed a number of Psalms on different occasions—as the need demanded. "In the night, His song shall be with you" (Psalm 42:8, NLT). "May the words of my mouth and the meditation

of my heart be pleasing to You, O Lord, my Rock and my Redeemer" (Psalm 19:4).

3. *Write the Psalm out to fully understand.* Did David write out his Psalms? Yes! How did we get them if he did not put them in words? He probably first memorized some Psalms, then wrote them out. Other Psalms he wrote out first, then committed them to memory. In the same way you should write out certain Psalms in your own words to make them more meaningful. "My son, do not forget My law, but let your heart keep My commands for length of days and long life...bind them around your neck, write them on the tables of your heart" (Proverbs 3:1-3, NKJV).

4. *Claim a promise.* You can sing a Psalm or claim it's promise when you are lonely or have deep needs, "I shall not want" (Psalm 23:1). When threatened physically, "I will fear no evil" (Psalm 23:4). When you doubt the future, "I will dwell in the house of the Lord forever" (Psalm 23:6).

5. *Use Psalms to worship God.* One of David 's strengths was worship—giving to God the total "worthship" He desires. Remember, Jesus told us, "The Father seeks worship" (John 4:23, ELT). If you have trouble worshiping God, use the Psalms that express David's praise. Then you will learn to praise God as David did. When David escaped Saul he wrote Psalm 18. "Therefore I will give thanks to You, O Lord, among the Gentiles, and sing praises to Your name" (Psalm 18:49).

6. *Apply restoration from sin as expressed in a Psalm.* "Have mercy upon me, O God, according to Your lovingkindness; according to the multitude of Your tender mercies, blot out my transgressions. For I acknowledge my transgressions, and my sin is always before me. Against You, You only, have I sinned, and done this evil in Your sight—that You may be found just when You speak, and blameless when You judge" (Psalm 51:1, 3-4).

7. *Realize you are wonderfully and fearfully made.* When did David realize the greatness of God's creation of man and woman? Probably he began learning about the source of life as a young shepherd with the birth of lambs. Then he continued learning with the birth of his children. "O Lord, You have searched me and known me. I will praise You, for I am fearfully and wonderfully made; marvelous are Your works, and that my soul knows very well" (Psalm 139:1, 14).

8. *When overwhelmed, thank God by using a Psalm.* "He delivers me from my enemies. You also lift me up above those who rise against me; You have delivered me from the violent man. Therefore I will give thanks to You, O Lord, among the Gentiles, and sing praises to Your name" (Psalm 18:48-49).

9. *Look at your deep feelings through the Psalm.* "As the deer pants for the water brooks, so pants my soul for You, O God. Why are you cast down, O my soul? And why are you disquieted within me? Hope in God; for I shall yet praise Him, the help of my countenance and my God" (Psalm 42:1, 11).

10. *Memorize and mediate the Psalms.* When did David begin memorizing Scriptures? We don't have any record, but probably he was memorizing as he re-sang each Psalm. It made an impression in his mind and influenced his morals. Also we don't know if David's mother taught him to memorize portions of Scriptures from Joshua and other passages in the Old Testament. Were they available to David in his day? But David's life was rich because he hid the treasures of Scriptures in his heart. "Your word I have hidden in my heart, that I might not sin against You" (Psalm 119:11).

Chapter 4

DAVID — FAITHFUL TO GOD'S CALLING

1 SAMUEL 23 TO 27

David the Fugative
(1 Samuel 19:18-27:12; Psalm 13; 34; 52; 54; 56-57; 63; 142)

DAVID the shepherd, who had become David the champion, was now David the fugitive. "So David fled and escaped, and went to Samuel at Ramah, and told him all that Saul had done to him" (1 Samuel 19:18). Soon word leaked back to the king that David was in Ramah with Samuel. Saul immediately sent men to Ramah to take David. But when the men arrived at Ramah and saw Samuel and a group of prophets prophesying, they too were overcome by the Spirit of God and began to prophesy.

When Saul learned what had happened, he sent a second group to accomplish the mission, but they too began to prophesy as they came to the city. The second group was followed by a third group which had the same thing happen to them. Finally, Saul himself went to Ramah to find David, and as he came near the place where David and Samuel were staying, he too began prophesying. Once again an earlier proverb from the life of Saul became a popular joke among the people, "Is Saul also among the prophets?" (v. 24).

DAVID AND JONATHAN

Perhaps remembering how Jonathan had earlier convinced Saul to preserve David's life, the fugitive left Ramah and appealed to Jonathan for help. Initially, Jonathan did not believe his father was involved in a plot against David's life, but agreed to protect David until the charge was proven. It was two days later that Saul realized his son Jonathan had helped David escape. The king's wrath was then directed toward his son. "Then Saul cast a spear at him to kill him, by which Jonathan knew that it was determined by his father to kill David" (20:33).

His father's attempt on his life left Jonathan in deep emotional turmoil. In anger, he stormed out of the room and refused to eat that day. That anger later turned to grief as he thought of his friend David who was the primary target of Saul's wrath. These emotions were mixed with a sense of shame, not only because he had been publicly humiliated by his father, but because his father had also humiliated him by his angry outburst. Also, Jonathan was torn apart emotionally, knowing he would have to separate himself from his dear friend in order to better protect him from his father.

The next day, David and Jonathan met according to their prearranged plan. In their moving moments together, two of the closest friend that have ever been, parted company. So emotionally charged was the atmosphere of that meeting that David wept uncontrollably for some time. As they parted, they renewed their promise of mutual friendship, not only for their lifetime on earth, but for eternity. For the rest of his life, Saul would spend much of his time hunting for David to kill him. And for the rest of his life, Jonathan would be loved more by David than by any other person on earth.

While David's years wandering as a fugitive from Saul were trying times for the man who would be king, this was also an era in his life when many of the psalms were written. While many of the psalms were difficult to place in a definite historical context with absolute certainty, there are several in which contextual titles or details within the psalms themselves suggest the historic background of their composition.

Just as on at least two occasions David escaped direct attempts on his life because Saul hurled a javelin at him, so David had at least two occasions in which there could be no question that David could have killed Saul had that been his desire (24:4; 26:7-12). On both occasions, David's close advisors urged David to kill Saul, arguing the act would have been in harmony with God's promise to give David the throne. But on both occasions, David refused to lay his hand against the one God had anointed as king of Israel. Ironically, it was in a battle with the Philistines, the very enemy of Israel which Saul had hoped would kill David, that King Saul and his son Jonathan would both die. Saul's constant pursuit of David over a period of more than a decade had actually driven David into Philistine territory for protection.

DAVID IN A CAVE AT EN-GEDI

David and his men were hiding in the caves of En-gedi, on the rocky shores of the Dead Sea. The water of the Dead Sea were too salty to drink, but there was a crystal clear pool of water at En-gedi, a perfect place for David's camp.

Saul had collected three thousand men to hunt for David and his group of men. They searched the mountains strongholds around En-gedi where they were hiding. When Saul and his party reached a cave, he went in to relive himself. Little did he realize that David and his own soldiers were hidden in smaller cavern leading off the main one.

Some of David 's men whispered to him that now was his change to kill Saul. "He (David) said to his men, 'The Lord forbid that

I should do this to my lord the king...the Lord's anointed one'" (1 Samuel 24:6, NLT).

But David did not wish to kill Saul. Instead, he crept into the main cave and secretly cut off a corner of Saul's robe.

Saul went on his way. David ran to the entrance and shouted after him. "Look...what I have in my hand...the hem of your robe!...I didn't kill you'" (1 Samuel 24:11, NLT). Then he asked Saul why he kept on listening to men and believing that David wanted to harm him. If he had wished to hurt Saul, could he have killed him there in the cave? But all he had done was cut off a corner from Saul's robe.

When Saul heard David's words he wept, saying: "Is that your voice, David, my son? You are more righteous than I am. You have behaved well toward me, but I have treated you badly. Today, when you could have killed me, you spared my life. May the Lord reward you greatly for the way you have dealt with me. But please promise me that when you become king, which I am sure will happen, you will not be unkind to my family, and will spare their lives" (1 Samuel 24:16-21, ELT).

David gave his word, and then Saul went home.

DAVID AGAIN SPARED SAUL'S LIFE

Several years passed. During this time the prophet Samuel—the one who anointed David—died. It was then the men of Ziph told Saul that "David was hiding on the hill of Hakilah" (1 Samuel 26:1).

So Saul led another army of three thousand men to search for David in the wilderness of Ziph. From his hiding place David watched them set up their great camp near the hill of Hakilah. That night David and Abishai one of his warriors, slipped through the dark to Saul's camp. "The Lord had put Saul's men into a deep sleep" (1 Samuel 26:12, NLT).

They crept through the ranks of sleeping soldiers until they came to the middle of the camp. They found Saul sleeping in the middle of a circle of carriages and chariots. Abner, Saul's general, and the men of the king's royal bodyguard were surrounding Saul.

As the two brave men slipped to Saul's side, Abishai whispered to David, "Now God had delivered him to you. Just let me pin him to the earth with my spear. It will not need doing a second time" (1 Samuel 26:8, NLT) But David answered, "No, we have no right to touch the Lord's anointed" (v. 11). Saul's spear was stuck nearby in the ground and his water bottle. David and Abishai carried them away.

David stood on a hilltop a distance from Saul's camp and shouted across to the soldiers and Abner. "Abner, why don't you do your duty to look after the king? In the night two of the king's enemies were right at his side. If they wished, they could have killed him. See, we have Saul's spear and water bottle" (v. 15-16, ELT).

King Saul recognized David's voice, and he cried out, "Is that you , my son, David?" (v. 17). David answered, "why do you hunt me, my lord? What have I done? If others have set you against me, my God will deal with them" (v. 18-19, ELT). David explained he could have killed Saul, but did not do it. Saul was sorry once more for what he had done, and confessed that he had sinned.

TEN WAYS TO BE FAITHFUL TO GOD'S CALLING FOR YOUR LIFE

1. *It's never right to do wrong things, even if you think you are right.* David had two opportunities to take Saul's life. First in the cave of En Gedi, and second in the plane of Hachilah. On both occasions, one of the warriors with David urge him to kill Saul. If

David killed Saul would he have gotten the throne the way God wanted to give it to him? Even though God had promised David the throne, it would have been wrong to kill Saul to become king. On both occasions David said he would not touch "God's anointed." That showed David's deep commitment to God who also anointed him.

When you enter a new position of leadership in ministry, don't enter it through the door of compromise, sin, lies, or break God's laws. God blessed David for his commitment to integrity and He will do the same for you.

2. *It is important to have witnesses for the good things you do.* When David refused to drive a spear into Saul's sleeping body, one of his warriors with him witnessed his integrity. It would have been satisfying to David to take the spear, perhaps the one Saul used to try to kill David and plunge it into Saul's body; but David's integrity ruled the day.

    In the same way, when you become a leader, you should "recompense to no man evil for evil...average not yourselves, but rather give place to wrath" (Romans 12:17-19). David had followers who watched him show mercy to Saul. Probably, they told the other followers of David, hence strengthening David's leadership position; but most of all, David gained more favor in God's sight and received more blessing in return.

3. *Always remember God's promises that put you in office/ministry.* God choose David as king. "Samuel took oil...and anointed him(David)" (1 Samuel 16:130. David was always mindful that God chose him, and that memory guided his life's activities. In the same way, remember God has led you and you are in ministry by God's choice.

4. *Follow God's providential open doors/situations.* There are many caves at En Gedi, (I have been there to walk in some of them), but God led Saul into a cave not knowing David was hiding in the rear of the cave. Because it was dark, David was able to secretly cut off part of Saul's garment. Afterwards when David held up the cut off piece of garment, it gave evidence to David's integrity. Saul missed the message from God. In the Hachilah open areas, David sneaked into Saul's camp to take his spear and water jug. Again David revealed his integrity. When you assume a leadership position in ministry, watch for opportunities when God can use an "open door" to demonstrate your integrity (1 Corinthians 16:9).

5. *Don't be swayed by bad advice from good people.* When David was hiding in the En Gedi cave, his men said to him, "This is the day of which the Lord said to you, 'Behold, I will deliver your enemy into your hand'" (1 Samuel 24:4). But David did not try to kill Saul. Then on the plane of Hachilah, Abishai wanted to drive Saul's spear into his body. But David again said, "Destroy him not; for who can stretch forth his hand against the Lord's anointed" (1 Samuel 26:9). The integrity of David's heart made him reject the pressure of his followers to kill Saul. When you become a leader, get your marching orders from God and His holy Word. Don't be intimated by suggestions from your friends or followers when their advice is contrary to God's Word.

6. *Always be guided by what you know is right.* David walked with God who was his Shepherd (Psalm 23). His Psalms were written about God, or sung and prayed to God. These influenced David's thinking and attitude towards life. In difficult circumstance, David did the right thing because it was what he knew to do.

7. *Don't retaliate.* Saul had hurled his spear at David in an attempt to kill him. "Saul sought to pin David to the wall with his spear" (1 Samuel 19:10). David didn't retaliate, David returned the spear to Saul on the plane of Hachilah late one night.

8. *Keep safe distance.* Even through David did not try to retaliate against Saul to hurt or kill him, David put distance between him and Saul. Who knows what a person in Saul's mental condition might do to David. At En Gedi, after Saul left, "David came out of the cave" (1 Samuel 24:2). On the plane of Hachilah, "David went over to the other side" (1 Samuel 26:13). There are some people in ministry you don't want too close to you. Yes you will deal with them, and you will work with them, but David would later write, "Blessed is the man that walketh not in the counsel of the ungodly, nor standeth in the way of sinners, nor sitteth in the seat of the scornful" (Psalm 1:1). Note the acerated distance...walking...standing...sitting. Then notice the accurate descending deception...ungodly...sinners...scorners. Why dose God tell us to keep our distance? Perhaps two reasons. First, associating with them will harm our testimony. Second, associating with them may influence us to do or say the same thing.

9. *Accept apologies, but be careful.* Twice Saul apologized to David. In En Gedi David came out of the cave to confront Saul. When Saul realize David could have killed him, the king said, "You *are* more righteous than I; for you have rewarded me with good, whereas I have rewarded you with evil" (1 Samuel 24:17). But even with the apology, David didn't go home with Saul. "Saul went home, but David and his men went up to the stronghold" (1 Samuel 24:22). At the plan of Hachilah, Saul apologized, "I have sinned. Return, my son David. For I will harm you no more, because my life was precious in your eyes this day. Indeed I have played the fool and erred exceedingly" (1 Samuel 26:21). Yet, David did not go home

with Saul. "David went on his way, and Saul returned to his place" (1 Samuel 26:25).

10. *Pray for your attackers and those who criticized you.* Jesus told us to "pray for those who despitefully use you" (Matthew 5:44). David sang his Psalm of thanksgiving for being delivered from evil men. He also sang Psalm 56:11-13 of praise to God and keeping his safe.

"In God I have put my trust;
I will not be afraid.
What can man do to me?

Vows made to You are binding upon me,
O God;
I will render praises to You,

For You have delivered my soul from death.
Have You not kept my feet from falling,
That I may walk before God
In the light of the living?"

Chapter 5

DAVID—FAITHFUL
AS A NEW KING

DAVID

The King
2 Samuel 1:1-10:19, Psalms 30; 60

ON the death of Saul, David was the king designated by God to lead God's people. But as is often the case, there was a period of confusion following the death of Saul. David was living in a foreign country which had defeated Israel and killed Saul. Therefore, he was not immediately accepted as king. One of the sons of Saul, Ishbosheth, was able to secure enough support to establish a rival reign as king over the northern tribes of Israel for seven and a half years.

David had only been back in the Holy Land a few days when he heard of the deaths of Saul and his dear friend Jonathan. David was approached by a young man with torn clothes and dust on his head. When the man saw David, he fell on his face before him and "prostrated himself' (2 Sam. 1: 2). When asked where he had come from, the man responded, "I have escaped from the camp of Israel" (v. 3).

Even though David was living in the land of the enemy and under their protection, he still had a deep love for his people Israel and realized he would someday rule over them. But his own problems with the Amalekites had kept him occupied during the most recent Israel-Philistia conflict and he had not yet heard from his usual sources how the battle had gone. It was, therefore, only natural that he should ask this young soldier how the battle had gone.

As David listened to the young messenger, he heard how Israel had fled in the midst of the battle, resulting in the loss of many lives including both Saul and Jonathan. He was not prepared to accept the deaths of his king and his friend on the basis of one man's unsubstantiated testimony; so he began to probe further, asking the messenger how he could be certain the king and his son Jonathan were in fact dead.

The messenger told David an "eyewitness" account of the death of Saul and presented the crown and bracelet of Saul as proof of the king's death. In the process of telling the story, the messenger made several claims. First, he identified himself as an Amalekite, a surviving member of the tribe Saul had been commanded by God to destroy fourteen years earlier. Second, he claimed Saul had unsuccessfully tried to take his own life by leaning on his spear. He further claimed Saul had asked him for help, requesting the Amalekite kill him. Finally, he admitted to killing Saul and removing the king's crown and bracelet to bring them to David.

The testimony of the Amalekite appears to conflict with another account of the death of Saul, and this has created problems for some interpreters of Scripture. The two accounts can be harmonized in either one of two ways. First, some scholars argue Saul did try to commit suicide but failed. His armor bearer did not realize Saul had failed and responded by successfully taking his own life. Later, as Saul groaned in pain dying from both the fatal wounds of the archers and his own attempted suicide, he saw the Amalekite and had him finish the job. A second view of some scholars argues the Amalekite found the body of Saul after the battle and took the crown and bracelet to David. The story about killing Saul was created by the Amalekite in hopes of impressing David and receiving a reward. Those who hold this second view note it is highly unlikely an Amalekite would be fighting in the army of Israel, especially in light of the fact they were engaged in their own battle against Ziklag at the time.

David and his men responded in mourning for the loss of Israel. "And they mourned, and wept and fasted until evening for Saul and for Jonathan his son, for the people of the Lord, and for the house of Israel, because they had fallen by the sword" (v. 12). Then David responded to the Amalekite's own claim of responsibility by sentencing and executing the man for destroying the Lord's anointed. David himself had had opportunity to take the life of Saul, but had refused because God had anointed Saul king of Israel. It is interesting to note David's observation, "Your blood is on your own head, for your own mouth has testified against thee, saying, `I have killed the Lord's anointed' " (v. 16). This does not mean the Amalekite was necessarily guilty, only that he had made a claim that caused him to appear guilty.

DAVID'S REIGN IN HEBRON

2 Samuel 2:1-5:12; Psalm 30

When David learned of the deaths of Saul and Jonathan, he "inquired of the Lord, saying, `Shall I go up to any of the cities of Judah?' " (2 Sam. 2:1) He knew Samuel had anointed him as king and successor to Saul, but there had always been a question of timing in David's mind. He had assumed God would remove Saul from the throne when the time was right, but before returning to Judah, David wanted to be certain. God assured David he was to return to Hebron with his men. When David settled in Hebron, "the men of Judah came, and there they anointed David king over the house of Judah" (v. 4).

As David became king of Judah, he learned it was the men of Jabesh Gilead who had buried the bodies of Saul and his sons who had been slain in battle. David sent a messenger to the men of that city expressing his own appreciation to them for what they had done and encouraged them as the newly anointed king of Judah. But it would be seven and a half years before that city and others of the north would become a part of David's kingdom.

Abner, Saul's former captain of the host, remained loyal to the dynasty of Saul and established a surviving son of Saul, Ishbosheth, on the throne of Israel as king. With the single exception of the tribe of Judah (which had anointed David as its king), Israel recognized Ishbosheth as their new king and followed him.

The names of the sons of Saul illustrate how far this king had wandered from his recognition of the true God of Israel. His oldest son Jonathan was named in recognition that Jehovah answers prayer. His second son was named Ishuai (Ishvi) probably because of some physical resemblance to his father. He is also called Abinadab (1 Chron. 8:33), which expressed Saul's willingness to serve the Lord. But by the birth of his third son, Saul had turned from the Lord to himself as the source of the nation's salvation. Ultimately, he was naming his sons after the idols which so often caused Israel to wander from God. When Saul died in battle, his oldest sons died with him, representing his testimony concerning God and himself. All that remained was his shame.

SONS OF SAUL

Jonathan—Jehova has given

Ishuai (Abinadab)—Resembling (willingness)

Malchishua—The king is salvation

Esh-Baal (Ishbosheth)—Man of Baal (shame)

Having two kings in Israel was bound to create problems, so it is not surprising that much of David's reign in Hebron involved him in a civil war. The war began at a meeting of the two armies by the pool of Gibeon. It appears the meeting was intended to be a peaceful meeting of the two sides until Joab, David's general, and his men took twelve of Abner's men and killed them with their own swords. "And there was a very fierce battle that day, and Abner and the men of Israel were beaten before the servants of David" (2 Sam. 2:17). At the end of the battle, Judah had recorded 19 casualties. Abner's men had lost 360.

So severe was the battle that day that the men of Israel were soon scattered and fleeing the battle. Among those on the run was Abner himself. As he escaped the battlefield, he was pursued by Asahel, the brother of Joab. Even at this point in the battle, Abner apparently believed Joab could be trusted. He pled with Asahel to stop pursuing him, claiming he did not want to kill him in self-defense as it would hinder relations between Joab and himself. But Asahel did not listen and finally Abner was forced to defend himself. Taking the butt end of his spear, Abner hit Asahel, probably intending to wind him so that he could escape. But the spear penetrated Asahel's chest cavity and Joab's brother died.

Despite the severe defeat Israel had that day, it marked the beginning rather than the end of the long war between the two kings.

During that period, there was a gradual strengthening of David's men and weakening of Abner's men. At times it seemed as though the war would continue without end. Then something happened between Ishbosheth and Abner that resulted in events which led to a quick end to the conflict.

Ishbosheth accused Abner of being involved with Rizpah, one of the concubines of Saul. In the context of those times, the charge amounted to that of treason and sedition. When a rebel wanted to usurp a throne, he would most often engage in relations with the wives and concubines of the king to demonstrate his authority over the throne. Abner had become increasingly stronger in the kingdom, and Ishbosheth, like his father before him, was becoming suspicious of a potential rival to the throne. There is no indication that there was any foundation for the charge against Abner.

Abner was understandably upset with Ishbosheth's accusation. He reminded the king of his loyalty to the dynasty of Saul and pointed out that he had not betrayed Ishbosheth to David despite apparent opportunities to do so. In his rage, Abner declared God would transfer the kingdom to David from Saul. Ishbosheth was stunned and scared into silence, "because he feared him" (3:11).

For over seven years, Abner had been loyal to Ishbosheth, not only establishing him on the throne but also fighting on his king's behalf and defending him from Joab. But the false charge of Ishbosheth against him turned his loyalty from the dynasty of Saul to a new dynasty of David. Abner sent a message to David requesting a treaty of peace be made between them. David agreed on the condition that his first wife, Michal, the daughter of Saul, be brought to him.

Though David was a man after God's own heart and followed the commandments of the Lord in most areas of his life, his greatest failures in life related to his family relations. This was in part due to his failure to apply biblical principles to this area of his life. Rather than adopt the biblical pattern of monogamy, David acquired at least eight wives and eleven concubines during his lifetime. In requesting here to be reunited with his first wife, he was also violating a biblical principle. Under the law, if a wife acquired another husband after a period of separation from her husband, it was viewed as an "abomination before the Lord" if she went back to the first husband (Dent. 24:4). Later, Michal would become a source of irritation to David.

David made his league with Abner, in effect uniting the kingdom under his leadership. After establishing a peace with Abner, David sent him away to gather Israel in peace. But not everyone was happy with David's actions. Joab was still bitter over the fact that Abner had killed his brother Asahel. Joab went into a tirade over David's decision to make peace with Abner. After expressing his opinion to David, Joab left the king's presence to take matters into his own hands. Without consulting David, "he sent messengers after Abner, who brought him back from the well of Sirah" (2 Sam. 3:26).

When Abner returned to Hebron, Joab was there to meet him. "Joab took him aside in the gate to speak with him privately, and there stabbed him in the stomach, so that he died for the blood of Asahel his brother" (v. 27). When David later learned of the death of Abner at the hand of Joab, he strangely lamented, "Should Abner die as a fool dies?" (v. 33) Despite the strange words, David's fasting and mourning of that day convinced the people he was sincere in his sense of loss for his friend and that the plot to kill Abner had not been initiated by the king.

David's comment concerning Abner's dying as a fool dies should be understood in the context of the cities of refuge in Israel. If a man took the life of another by accident, he was safe from relatives of the deceased who might seek vengeance only so long as he remained in a city of refuge. Hebron was one of the six cities of refuge. Joab could not take the life of Abner until he "took him aside in the gate" (v. 27). At the time of his death, Abner was literally steps away from safety. Some commentators see Abner in his death as a picture of the unsaved man in conviction who "comes to the gate" but never takes the step of saving faith and trusts Christ to save him.

The death of Abner left Ishbosheth and his people in a state of confusion, disarray, and fear. Two of Ishbosheth's own captains plotted a coup and killed their king as he slept in bed during the heat of the day. Traveling by night, they took the head of Ishbosheth to David in Hebron, probably expecting to be rewarded for their efforts. But David was not at all impressed with the murder of "a righteous person in his own house on his bed" (4:11). Baanah and Rechab, the men who had killed Ishbosheth, were executed by David for the murder of their king. David took the head of Ishbosheth and "buried it in the tomb of Abner" (v. 12).

The death of Ishbosheth left Israel without a king. The elders of Israel had already discussed the possibility of making David their king when Abner had defected, and now took that course of action. The kingdom was again reunited and David was anointed king over all Israel. This was the third time David had been anointed as a king.

With the civil war resolved, David turned his attention to the city of Jerusalem. The Jebusites thought they were secure in their city, so much so that they claimed even the blind and the lame could defend it. But David took the city. Joab climbed up the water shaft, a tunnel under the wall by which water was brought into the city. David then made that city his capital for the remaining years of his reign. Even to this day, Jerusalem is sometimes called "the city of David." He lived in the fort of the city until carpenters and masons from his ally Hiram, king of Tyre, finished building his palace. "So David knew that the Lord had established him as king over Israel, and that He had exalted his kingdom for His people Israel's sake" (5:12). At the dedication of his palace, David wrote a psalm of thanksgiving and praise for what God had done for him (Ps. 30).

DAVID'S REIGN IN JERUSALEM

2 Samuel 5:13-10:19; Psalm 60

Jerusalem was already important in Israel's history even before it was conquered by David. Melchizedek, to whom Abraham had paid tithes, was king of (Jeru)Salem (Gen. 14:18). In conquering this city, David acquired this dynastic title "a priest forever according to the order of Melchizedek" which later was ascribed to Jesus (cf. Ps. 110:4). Also, Jerusalem was the place where Abraham nearly offered his son Isaac to God in a burnt offering. Being built on a hill, the city was visible from Bethlehem, and David may have dreamed of conquering it even as a boy in Bethlehem.

After establishing his throne in Jerusalem, David fought and defeated the enemy of Israel which Saul had neglected while pursuing David. He finished the task begun by Samson "and drove back the Philistines from Geba [Gibeon) as far as Gezer" (2 Sam. 5:25).

As Moses had prepared Israel to conquer the land, he told the people God would establish a central place of worship once they had settled the land (cf. Deut. 12). God would not confirm that place until the dedication of Solomon's temple, but David realized it was time to bring the ark of the covenant to Jerusalem. Perhaps his defeat of the Philistines caused him to remember how they had transported the ark back to Israel on a cart (1 Sam. 6:7-8). David, therefore, chose that method to carry the ark to Jerusalem despite the fact God had already instructed how the ark should be carried (cf. Num. 4:5-15).

Though David's intentions were honorable, he tried to do a right thing in a wrong way, and the result led to the death of a man named Uzzah. As the cart shifted, Uzzah reached for the ark to prevent it from falling, but God killed him as he touched the side of the ark. Fearful and angry over the death of Uzzah, David stopped the journey of the ark and had it removed from the cart and carried it into the home of Obed-Edom the Gittite. The ark remained there for three months before David resumed the project of taking it to Jerusalem.

This time the ark was carried by men, and the spirit of the occasion was once again festive. Those who bore the ark had only begun the journey when David began offering his sacrifices. In his enthusiasm at the time, "David danced before the Lord with all his might; and David was wearing a linen ephod" (2 Sam. 6:14).

When Michal, Saul's daughter and David's first wife, saw David dancing in the clothes of a commoner before God, she was offended at her husband's willingness to set aside his regal robes on such an occasion. Sarcastically, she met her husband with the words, "How glorious was the king of Israel today, uncovering himself today in the eyes of the maids of his servants, as one of the base fellows shamelessly uncovers himself!" (v. 20) The uncalled-for remark marked a breach in David's relations with his wife. He made it clear he would humble himself before God willingly, even if he appeared contemptible to the queen. "Therefore, Michal the daughter of Saul had no children to the day of her death" (v. 23).

SEVEN PRINCIPLES
TO ENTER A NEW POSITION

1. *Know God has chosen and appointed you.* There were many obstacles and closed doors for David to become king. Even at the beginning Samuel looked at David 's seven older brothers before anointing David. Then David faced opposition (both subtle and violent) from Saul. David spent the last of his teen years and all of his twenties in exile, being chased by Saul. Even after Saul's death, it took another seven years before the northern tribes

recognized David as king. Yet all this time David knew in his heart God had anointed him king.

As you take a position of leadership in ministry, first you must realize God wants you in that position. Then second, apply the laws of finding God's will to make sure God has lead you thus far. There will always be opportunities to lead. Sometimes opportunities are generated in life by satan who wants to destroy God's work. Sometimes it comes from people who have questions about your leadership, questions that may be legitimate to them, but not necessarily to you.

But in spite of opportunities, closed doors and circumstances, you must know God is leading you. Then, push ahead in the confidence that God has appointed you to the position. Just as David prayed, "Shall I go up" (2 Samuel 2:1), before assuming the throne, you must pray about the move, and seek God's guidance.

2. *David got the support and approval of his followers.* He didn't attempt to be king as a "lone eagle," assuming the position by himself without support. "David took...two wives...the men who were with him...with their households" (2 Samuel 2:2-3). When you have the opportunity to assume a new position/ministry, make sure your team of supporters are on board. You need their presence, their support and their help in your new challenge.

3. *Pray for those not chosen.* When David approached the crown, he was sensitive to Saul and his sons who night have laid claim to the throne. The Scriptures gives the account of David's prayer for them (2 Samuel 1:17-27).

4. *Identify with those you will lead.* David was finally anointed king over the northern tribes (those that previously rejected David

for Saul's line) David identified with those who initially rejected him because they were Hebrews, i.e., children of Abraham. David was able to untie the two sections together. Those from the north said, "We are your own flesh and blood" (2 Timothy 5:1, NLT).

You cannot lead a part of the "body of Christ" if they perceive you are an outsider, whether this is a denomination and distinction, or lifestyle difference. The group you are attempting to lead must feel one with you. How will that happen? You must take the initiative by identifying with them.

5. *Find a permeant home for ministry.* David did this by placing his center of operation in a new location, making it the "heart" for ministry. Note—David did not locate himself in the southern tribe of Judah, nor in the northern tribe. "David took the stronghold of Zion (Jerusalem)...dwelt in the stronghold" (2 Samuel 5:7, 9, NKJV).

In the same sense of unifying all people under your leadership, find a center of operation for ministry where all your followers can identify with you and from this new base of ministry, they can follow your leadership.

6. *Be ready to defend.* When David become king over all Israel, his first order of business was dealing with the surrounding nations that had previously been hostile to Israel. "Philistines heard... David was king...they mobilized" (2 Samuel 5:17).

Like it or not, there will always be opposition to God's work. We will get opposition from the world, the flesh and the devil (1 John 2:15-17). Therefore, when you become a leader—expect opposition.

You won't spend all your time and energy fighting your opposition. But expect problems and be ready to solve them. At the same time you are dealing with your opposition, make sure you are building up your ministry, and looking after the needs of your followers.

7. *Put God at the center.* When you attempt the above principles of talking a new position/ministry put God at the center of all you do. When David began to consolidate his kingdom, "They brought the Ark of the Lord and sat it...inside the special tent David prepared" (2 Samuel 6:17, NLT). The Ark of the Lord was the location where the presence of God dwelt. When David put the Ark at the center of the kingdom, he put God there.

The work of God must always go forward, but there will always be attacks from without, as well as opposition from within. Therefore, apply the principles of David when assuming a new position of leadership. The clothes and customs of the people will change, but the principles of evil attacks against God's ministry will always be present. Therefore, use the principles of David to ensure God's blessings on your leadership in new ministry.

Chapter 6

DAVID—FAITHFUL TO REPENT AFTER TERRIBLE SIN

2 SAMUEL 11:1-24:25;
1 KINGS 1:1-2:11;
PSALMS 3; 7, 18; 72

GOD elevated David from the humble task of caring for sheep to the majesty of ruling Israel during a time of great national success and prosperity. But the prosperity of Israel during his reign was not just a chance happening. It was the blessing of God on "the man after God's own heart." David and his kingdom were honored by God because they honored God in all they did. Generations later it would be affirmed, "David did what was right in the eyes of the Lord, and had not turned aside from anything that He commanded him all the days of his life, except in the matter of Uriah the Hittite" (1 Kings 15:5).

The darkest hour of David's life began one sleepless night in Jerusalem. Israel was again at war, and again Israel was winning. They were defeating the Ammonites and had laid siege to the city of Rabbah. It was largely a waiting game now, and David had decided to wait it out in his own bed in Jerusalem rather than to go to the battlefield with his men. In fact, he had suspected Ammon would not be much of an enemy to defeat, so he had sent his men to fight under Joab while he himself remained in his palace. But he just couldn't get to sleep one night no matter how hard he tried. Maybe some fresh air would help, so he went to the roof of his house to walk about.

BATHSHEBA:
THE WIFE OF URIAH THE HITTITE

(2 Samuel 11:1-27)

It was while he was standing on the roof that he first saw Bathsheba. She was bathing at the time and the absence of clothing only served to accentuate her physical beauty. As David continued watching, he began asking questions. He learned her name was Bathsheba, the wife of one of the thirty-seven elite military commanders identified as "David's mighty men." He knew her husband Uriah well. Uriah had proved himself a soldier of excellence on the battlefield where it counted. And he knew where Uriah was at the time—camped out in Ammon waiting for the city of Rabbah to fall.

No longer was David interested in trying to get to sleep. It was Bathsheba who now captivated his mind. Watching her bathe at a distance, he decided to bring her closer. It would be less conspicuous if she were to come to the palace than if he were to go to her home, so he sent a messenger to summon her to his presence. There in the ornate palace and in the presence of her respected and beloved king, she succumbed to his improper advances. They found themselves sharing a common bed betraying an honorable husband and faithful friend. By morning Bathsheba had returned home, and no one had to know what had taken place. But Bathsheba had conceived, and very soon thereafter both she and her king realized they had a problem to resolve.

The advantage of being king is that there are times you can pull strings and do things no one else could do. David was sure he had a plan that was guaranteed to work. It was about time he got another report from the battle and he would call Uriah to return with the report. He would return to Jerusalem, spend a few nights with his wife, then return to the battle where he was needed. How could Uriah resist the charms of his lovely wife! When she later gave birth to her child, Uriah would remember the weekend he had come home from the battle and simply assume he had fathered the child.

But Uriah was a disciplined soldier who would not allow himself to enjoy the simple pleasures of life when there was a battle to be won. Though his home was in the city, Uriah insisted on sleeping at the door of his king's palace. "The ark and Israel and Judah are dwelling in tents," he explained, "and my lord Joab and the servants of my lord are encamped in the open fields. Shall I then go to my house to eat and to drink, and to be with my wife? As you live, and as your soul lives, I will not do this thing" (2 Sam. 11:11). Uriah's statement amounted to an oath sworn on the life of his king.

David did not have much time to act. He knew Bathsheba would begin to show evidences of her condition soon and he did not want to find himself in the midst of a moral scandal. He decided to try again. He invited Uriah to be his guest at a banquet the next night and made sure Uriah was drunk before he left. But even in his drunken state, he did not return home to his wife but remained at the palace. It was time for David to initiate his alternative approach to resolving the problem.

The next morning, David sent Uriah back to the battle with sealed orders for Joab. Uriah was to be sent on a suicide mission which would attempt to storm the walls of Rabbah. David made it clear to Joab he wanted to receive the report of Uriah's death. Though Uriah had held the life of his king in high regard, David counted the life of Uriah as expendable in covering his sin. The storming of the walls was a disaster for Israel, but a success for David. Several soldiers lost their lives in the battle, including one named Uriah, the Hittite. When Bathsheba learned of the death of her husband, she mourned as was expected. "And when her mourning was over, David sent and brought her to his house, and she became his wife and bore him a son. But the thing that David had done displeased the Lord" (v. 27).

David had covered his tracks, but he was unable to shake the guilt of his sin. Throughout the whole ordeal of trying to cover his sin, there was a recurring fear that what he had done might be discovered and exposed. The growing guilt and fear combined to age him physically and cause him much discomfort. Later David himself confessed, "When I kept silent, my bones grew old through my groaning all the day long. For day and night Your hand was heavy upon me; my vitality is turned into the drought of summer" (Ps. 32:3-4). But the inner conviction of sin in David's heart failed to bring this king to repentance. Now it was time for God to initiate His alternative approach to resolving the problem.

NATHAN: THE PROPHET OF COURAGE AND CREATIVITY

(2 Samuel 12:1-31; Psalm 51)

"Then the Lord sent Nathan to David" (2 Sam. 12:1). Nathan had the difficult task of calling a popular yet unrepentant king to repentance. Much had already been done to hide the sin that had been committed and Nathan had been informed by God that David had arranged the death of Uriah. If the king was willing to kill one of his most trusted soldiers and able to cover his sin, certainly he would not stop at killing a prophet also. Even before Nathan arrived at the palace that day, he knew he was taking a course of action that could endanger his life. He also knew if he was going to be successful at turning his king back to God, he would have to be creative in his approach to the king.

God had brought David out from the sheepfold to lead Israel as king, but he had never taken the shepherd out of David. Therein was Nathan's hope of success. As he appeared before the king, he asked for the king's opinion concerning the matter of a stolen sheep. David listened intently as Nathan explained how a poor man had only one sheep and had cared for it as best he could. Then he heard how a rich man with a large flock of sheep and herd of cattle stole the poor man's sheep to feed a guest he was entertaining rather than have to give up one of his own sheep. David's blood began to boil as he heard of the mercenary actions of the rich man. The man deserved to die, the king concluded, but not before he restored the stolen lamb fourfold.

Emphatically, Nathan seized the moment. "You are the man," he declared (v. 7). With piercing eyes Nathan looked at the fearful king and declared the accusation of the Lord. God had given David much and had been willing to give David much more if he wanted it, but David had stepped over the line in the matter of Uriah, the Hittite. He was guilty of murder and guilty of adultery, and there would be a severe price to pay for his sin. Briefly Nathan reviewed what David's sin would cost the fallen king. There would be no hiding this time, "for you did it secretly, but I will do this thing before all Israel, before the sun" (v. 12).

PROPHETIC WOE

1. Sword will never depart your home

2. Evil will rise from within

3. Your wives will be taken

4. Enemies will blaspheme you

David himself had called for the stolen sheep to be repaid fourfold, and that was the price David would have to pay. In the months and years to come, David would see his own children victimized and suffer as a consequence of his night with Bathsheba and subsequent covering of his sin. A baby would die. A daughter would be raped by her own brother who would then be killed by another son. As David lost the moral leadership of the land, one of his own sons would lead a coup strong enough to send David running from his own palace. The consequence of this sin would run its course until the fourfold punishment was paid in full. The mighty King David was powerless to control these circumstances. There was nothing he could do but watch the events unfold in the years to come, and contemplate the serious consequences and severe penalty of sin. Before his account was stamped "paid in full," there would be tears and anger, sadness and fear. Not even the king was above the Law of God.

FOURFOLD PAYMENT

1. Death of infant son

2. Rape of Daughter Tamar

3. Murder of Amnon

4. Death of Absalom

It was time for David to stop trying to hide his sin and begin dealing with it. As he turned back to God in repentance, he prayed what has since become one of the most beloved of all of the psalms. "Have mercy upon me, O God, according to Your loving-kindness; according to the multitude of Your tender mercies, blot out my transgressions" (Ps. 51:1). In the course of his prayer, David traveled the seven successive steps back to the place of full communion with and service for God. When David repented, Nathan reported a second message from heaven. "The Lord also has put away your sin; you shall not die" (2 Sam. 12:13).

Though God forgave David, there were still problems. "However, because by this deed you have given great occasion to the enemies of the Lord to blaspheme, the child also that is born to you shall surely die" (v. 14). Nathan left the palace, but before long David received word his youngest son was extremely sick. For a week he prayed and fasted to the Lord for the child, but the child's condition only got worse.

SEVEN STEPS
BACK TO COMMUNION WITH GOD

1. Sin thoroughly judged before God (Ps. 51:1-6)

2. Forgiveness through the blood (v. 7)

3. Cleansing (vv. 7-10)

4. Spirit-filled for joy and power (vv. 11-12)

5. Service (v. 13)

6. Worship (vv. 14-17)

7. The restored believer in fellowship with God

Night after night he went without sleep as he watched and prayed, but these were prayers that would be refused. So intense was his prayer for his sick child that his own servants feared to tell him when the child died. But when David realized the child was dead, he broke his fast and returned to a more normal lifestyle. He knew there was nothing he could do to bring the child back to life, and rested in the hope they would someday be reunited beyond the grave (2 Sam. 12:23).

The loss of a child was especially sorrowful to its mother. "Then David comforted Bathsheba his wife, and went in to her and lay with her. So she bore a son, and he called his name Solomon. And the Lord loved him" (v. 24). On the birth of Solomon to David and Bathsheba, Nathan returned with a different message than that which he had brought the previous year. He called Solomon, the newborn child, "Jedidiah," which means "beloved of the Lord." The birth of Solomon was a confirmation from God that the sin the couple had been involved in about two years previous was indeed forgiven by God.

But Israel was still fighting the battle at Rabbah. It was there David had sent Uriah on a suicide mission as he tried to cover his sin. Now that his sin had been forgiven and that forgiveness had been confirmed to him in the birth of Solomon, it was time to finally deal with the problem at Rabbah. Joab had finally cut off the water supply to the city and knew the end of the siege was very near. David gathered together his army and led them once more into battle. When they won the battle, David had a new crown of gold and gemstones along with other spoils of war added to his royal treasures. The Ammonites who survived the battle were enlisted by David as manual laborers for his continuing construction projects. "Then David and all the people returned to Jerusalem" (v. 31).

Though they would still experience complications in their lives stemming indirectly from the sin in which they had engaged, both David and Bathsheba realized a ministry in the lives of others born out of suffering they had experienced during that time and later. David's confession of sin became a favorite psalm among those familiar with the book, and Bathsheba trained her son to learn from his father's mistake. It is not surprising that her son would years later remember three particular lessons taught him by his mother during his formative years. First, he was not to give his "strength unto women, nor thy ways to that which destroyeth kings" (Prov. 31:3). Second, he was to avoid the use of wine or strong drink (vv. 4-7). Third, he should be quick to speak on behalf of and defend the cause of the poor and needy (vv. 8-9). The rest of his life might have been different if David had remembered these principles in his dealings with Uriah the Hittite.

TEN STEPS OF RESTORATION—PSALM 51

1. *Plead the mercy of God.* When a child of God chooses to sin, he/ she is hit with a great conviction of grief and condemnation. Sometimes when a person sins greatly and is not convicted of sin, it many means they are not saved. Or perhaps they may be backslidden and harden in heart that they do not feel guilt, or convicted of the personal agony when they offend God.

   When David sinned, apparently he did not feel the conviction of sin until Nathan the prophet of God pointed his accusing finger, "Thou art the man." It is then David repented and begged, "have mercy upon me...according to Your multitude of mercies" (Psalm 51:1-2).

2. *Thoroughly confess and repent of your sins.* When the truth of David's sin broke upon him, he confessed his sin, "My iniquity...I acknowledged my transgression" (Psalm 51:2-3). If you want God to thoroughly forgive your sins, then you must thoroughly confess it before the Lord. they just as thoroughly repent and turn from that sin. Sin is a hidden evil of the heart. So we must completely open our hearts to God, confess our sins and repent.

3. *Realize sin is primarily against God, secondarily against others, and lastly against you.* David prayed, "Against You, and You alone, have I sinned" (Psalm 51:4). When our sin is against our loved ones, we must apologize, repent, and beg for forgiveness. If your sin involves breaking a law of the city or state, you may have to pay a fine or serve time. The issue—sin always leads to consequences. Sometimes we must deal with the consequences, after we deal with God.

4. *Claim God's judgment against sin.* When David was begging God to forgive him, he prayed, "Your judgment against me is just" (Psalm 51:4). Remember God's forgiveness is based on His act of justification. "The blood of Jesus Christ His Son cleanses us from all sin" (1 John 1:7). In addition of cleansing of sin, God also cleanses the books of Heaven. Actual sin involves actual consequences, and they must be dealt with after God forgives you. But in Heaven, sin is charged to your account—this non-experiential guilt. It is on the record in Heaven. When Jesus died for our sins, He justified us. That means He cleansed the records in Heaven. Some have said that justification means, *just as if I had never sinned.* That is a play on words explaining the legal position in Heaven. But what about the cleaning of our mind and heart of the sin we committed? That is actual cleaning and restoration.

5. *Ask for cleansing.* David prayed, "Purge me...I shall be clean, wash me...whiter than snow" (Psalms 51:7). This is the experiential side of restoration. When we sin we feel bad—guilty—and we feel cut off from God—alienation. This is not about the legal aspect of our sin; this is the everyday feelings of isolation and shame. But God promised, "If we confess our sins; He is faithful and just to forgive us our sins, and cleanse us from all unrighteousness" (1 John 1:9).

6. *Remove sin completely.* This step is sometimes called repentance when we turn from our sins to God. Yes we turn to God, but the necessary part is also to turn from sin. This section says, *remove sin completely.* That has two actions. First, you remove yourself from the presence of sin, so you won't be tempted again. But second, you remove the presence of temptation or sin from your life. This means you leave it, and throw it away, or stay away.

    David prayed, "Hide Your face from my sin" (Psalm 51:9). God cannot look at sin, so get it out of His presence in your life and your environment. When you leave a room of sin, you leave it physically,

7. *Worship.* When David sinned, earlier you read he did not write or use a Psalm in worship. What did that absence say about David's spiritual condition? When David dealt with his sin he prayed, "My tongue shall sing...my lips shall praise" (Psalm 51:14). When David restored his fellowship with God he immediately began to worship. Remember, worship is about God, it centers your thoughts, desires and actions towards Him. When David began to worship, it restored his previous fellowship with God.

8. *Ask for spirit-filled joy and peace.* When there is sin in your life the Holy Spirit's ministry is blocked. When you confess your sin you release the Holy Spirit to minister to you and for you. He is called *Holy*, which means to separate from sin. The Holy Spirit is also *Spirit*. He is given to make you spiritual in your relationship with God. David prayed, for the Holy Spirit to restore..."the joy of Your salvation" (Psalm 51:11-12).

   One of the terrible spiritual consequences of your sin is the blockage of the Holy Spirit's working in your life. But when you deal with cleaning for your sins, you also release the Holy Spirit to work again in your life.

9. *Service.* Look at David's reaction to being restored to fellowship with God. "I will teach transgressors Your ways" (Psalm 51:13). Once you are in fellowship with God, you want to begin doing again what you lost when you sinned. You want to serve God. David as king was an example to all in Israel. Could it be said he was a teaching example of a godly life. He wanted that role badly. When you get restored, you will want to serve the Lord again.

10. *Enjoy restoration.* When David confessed his sin and was restored to fellowship, it was then he could say, "you shall be pleased with sacrifice" (Psalm 51:19). Do you think David made sacrifices to God after he sinned with Bathsheba? Would God accept David's sacrifice if sin wasn't confessed? What about David's sin against Uriah...manslaughter? Again, did God accept David's sacrifice if he did not confess then? But after the fall and tearful repentance, David approaches God the right way. Now he could pray, "You shall be pleased with sacrifice" (v. 19).

Chapter 7

DAVID—FAITHFUL AT THE END

THE LAST DAYS OF DAVID'S LIFE

THE last ten years of David's life were relatively peaceful, compared to the turmoil of the early years when he was chased by Saul. In David's early reign as king, he defended his nation against surrounding tribes or nations. Israel had conquered all the nations opposing her, and was at peace. There was no challenge to David's throne from within his family. Assyria, Babylon, and Egypt were weakened because of many contributing factors. Perhaps God was giving David ten years of peace to enjoy his last days on earth. Saul's house had been completely destroyed and David's dynasty was secure. David describe his last days in 2 Samuel 23:1-5, NKJV:

Now these are the last words of David.
Thus says David the son of Jesse;
  Thus says the man raised up on high,
The anointed of the God of Jacob,
  And the sweet psalmist of Israel:

"The Spirit of the Lord spoke by me,
  And His word was on my tongue.

The God of Israel said,
The Rock of Israel spoke to me:
'He who rules over men must be just,
Ruling in the fear of God.

And he shall be like the light of the morning when the sun rises,
A morning without clouds,
Like the tender grass springing out of the earth,
By clear shining after rain.'

"Although my house is not so with God,
Yet He has made with me an everlasting covenant,
Ordered in all things and secure.
For this is all my salvation and all my desire;
Will He not make it increase?

Did you see that statement describing David as "the sweet Psalmist of Israel?" And what were David's accomplishments? Can we say his greatest contribution was in his composition of songs/Psalms, as he left his heart in the pages of Scripture to touch the heart of people for 3,000 years? Can a man make a greater contribution than that?

Beyond his writings, David freed Israel from its enemies and established Israel as an autonomous nation. Also he unified the nation combing twelve tribes into one nation, and he ruled from a unified throne. He established Jerusalem as the capital, a decision that has remained throughout the centuries. Even to this day Jerusalem is considered the center of Israel's life. David established a Hebrew lifestyle in obedience to God and His Word. They sacrifice to God and both pleasing Him and honored Him. But beyond all this David became the ideal leader/patriarch, so that when succeeding generations thought of the coming Messiah, they would compare Him to David, actually calling Messiah, "the son of David."

FINDING THE SPOT FOR THE TEMPLE

2 Samuel 24; 1 Chronicles 21

David reigned undisturbed to the end of his days. During this time David decided to carry out a census numbering all the people in the land. Joab warned David that a census was against the commandment of God. God did not want His people to be filled with a feeling of their own greatness, and turn from trusting in Him.

However, David was stubborn and would not listen to Joab or the other captains of the army. They carried out his orders and numbered (a censes by counting heads) the people of all the tribes. It took nine months and twenty days, then they reported to David that in the whole land there were eight hundred thousand men able to bear arms, and of them five hundred thousand belonged to Judah. The tribes of Levi and Benjamin were not included.

Once the numbering was over, David began to worry. He had broken God's commandment, and pleaded to be forgiven for behaving foolishly. But it was too late.

Early one morning God sent Gad the prophet to David saying, "The Lord offers you three things. Either seven years of famine will come to the land, or three months your enemies will overrun the land, or three days of pestilence and terrible disease in the land." David didn't want seven years of famine and was afraid to fall into the hands of his enemies. He chose the three days of pestilence.

When it came it was terrible. In the three days, seventy thousand people died. In the end, the angel of death arrived at the gates of Jerusalem, and came to the threshing floor that belonged to Araunah the Jebusite.

At the time, King David saw the angel of the Lord standing between Heaven and earth, with his sword drawn and stretched out over

Jerusalem. Then David and the elders who were with him threw themselves down on their faces, begging God to take away the plague and spare Jerusalem. David prayed, "O God, I have sinned, and not my people. Let Your punishment come upon me and upon my family, but spare my people, who have done no wrong themselves."

Gad the prophet told David to go build an altar on the threshing floor of Araunah the Jebusite. David immediately obeyed. As David approached the spot, Araunah and his sons ran and bowed themselves down in front of their king.

David asked Araunah to name the price of the threshing floor, so that he could buy it to build the altar. At first Araunah wanted to donate the place to him, together with the oxen for burnt offerings, and the threshing instruments for firewood, and the wheat for a food offering. But David refused to take it without paying. This was his reason, "I must pay the full price, because I will not take somebody else's property for the Lord, nor offer Him burnt offerings without them costing me anything." So David paid six hundred shekels of gold for the place, and built his altar there. On the altar he arranged the firewood, and placed a special peace offerings and burnt offerings to the Lord.

The very next verse tells what happened after David made the sacrifice to God in Araunah's threshing floor. "Then David said, 'This will be the location for the Temple of the Lord God and the place of the altar for Israel's burnt offerings!'" (1 Chronicles 22:1, NLT).

THE CORONATION
OF SOLOMON

1 Kings 1:1-2:11; Psalm 72

As David approached the end of his life, he was weakened physically and spent much of his time in bed. While in this state, yet another attempt to seize David's throne was launched by one of his sons. Adonijah conferred with Joab and Abiathar the priest, and with their support tried to present himself to the nation as heir to his dying father's throne.

David had earlier promised Bathsheba their son Solomon would be the heir. When she learned of Adonijah's actions, she and Nathan approached David with the problem. David responded by ordering an immediate coronation of his son Solomon. Zadok the priest took oil from the tabernacle and anointed Solomon as king. Further they put Solomon on David's mule to ride into Jerusalem, a symbolic trip for the transfer of authority, from one king to the succeeding one. The trumpets announced the coronation. Then when the crown was placed on Solomon's head the transfer of authority was complete. Then Solomon would take his place on David's throne.

The action on the part of David led to widespread rejoicing as the people celebrated their new king. As part of the coronation celebration, David wrote what would be his final Psalm (Psalm 72).

SYMBOLS OF APPROVAL FOR KING

- Official blessing form high priest, 1:39
- Rode on king's symbol of power (David's mule), 1:38

- Crowned with king's symbol of power
- Official recognition (trumpets), 1:39
- Anointed at God's house—Tabernacle, 1:39
- Sit on throne, 1:35

Soon Adonijah and his followers heard the noise of the coronation and learned what it meant. "And all the guests who were with Adonijah were afraid, and arose, and each one went his way" (1 Kings 1:49). Solomon chose not to mar the celebration of that day by killing his adversaries but rather decided to give them a second chance to prove themselves.

DAVID PLANS THE TEMPLE IN JERUSALEM

With the Ark in Jerusalem and David in his palace, not having to fight enemies, it began to bother him that he should live in such comfortable surroundings, but the Ark should remain in a tent. He discussed the matter with Nathan the prophet who encouraged David to build the temple. But later that night, Nathan received a message directly from the Lord concerning that particular matter.

God wanted the prophet to deliver a message to the king. He was to remind David, "Thus says the Lord of hosts: `I took you from the sheepfold, from following the sheep, to be ruler over My people, over Israel'" (7:8). God blessed David, giving him rest from his enemies, but God did not want David building His temple. God established a covenant with David that would be the foundation of the government of the thousand-year reign of Christ. David's son and heir would be the builder of the temple. As much as David may have wanted to undertake this project, he would not be allowed by God to build the temple.

Rather than become frustrated over God's refusal to allow him to build a temple, David responded to Nathan's message from God with a prayer of humble thanksgiving to God for what He had already done for him and praise for who God is. If he could not build the temple, he would do what he could. By the end of David's life, he had designed the temple and gathered most of the materials needed for its building.

David had one last major task in life. God wanted him to prepare all the building materials and the workers for the building of the Temple, but it would be built under Solomon. "Then David gave his son Solomon the plans for the vestibule, its houses, its treasuries, its upper chambers, its inner chambers, and the place of the mercy seat; and the plans for all that he had by the Spirit, of the courts of the house of the Lord, of all the chambers all around, of the treasuries of the house of God, and of the treasuries for the dedicated things...'All this,' said David, 'the Lord made me understand in writing, by His hand upon me, all the works of these plans'" (1 Chronicles 28:11-12, 19, NKJV). David had received the full instructions concerning the design of the temple, how everything was to be placed together, nothing was to be left to chance.

Originally God had told David that he could not build the temple because he was a man of war, "The word of the Lord came to me, saying, 'You have shed much blood and have made great wars; you shall not build a house for My name, because you have shed much blood on the earth in My sight" (1 Chronicles 22:8, NKJV).

It was obvious that Solomon was to build the Temple. God told David, "Behold, a son shall be born to you, who shall be a man of rest; and I will give him rest from all his enemies all around. His name shall be Solomon, for I will give peace and quietness to Israel in his days. He shall build a house for My name, and he shall be My son, and I will be his Father; and I will establish the throne of his kingdom over Israel forever.

Now, my son, may the Lord be with you; and may you prosper, and build the house of the Lord your God, as He has said to you" (1 Chronicles 22:9-11, NKJV). Obviously, God was talking about building the first Temple, but God also had in mind that David would eventually have another son many generations away, who would build the Temple/church (Ephesians 2). That son would be name Jesus Christ. Jesus would build a house, i.e., the church.

Notice the wisdom of David as he turned the task of building the Temple over to Solomon as well as the kingdom. "My son Solomon, whom alone God has chosen, is young and inexperienced; and the work is great, because the Temple is not for man but for the Lord God" (1 Chronicles 29:1, NKJV).

Notice the commitment that David made in building the Temple. "I am donating more than 112 tons of gold from Ophir and 262 tons of refined silver to be used for overlaying the walls of the buildings and for the other gold and silver work to be done by the craftsmen" (1 Chronicles 29:4-5, NLT).

Then the text goes on to describe how big the Temple would be. Beyond that, David instructs all the family leaders to donate to the construction of the Temple. "For the construction of the Temple of God, they gave about 188 tons of gold, 10,000 gold coins, 375 tons of silver, 675 tons of bronze, and 3,750 tons of iron" (1 Chronicles 29:7, NLT).

What can be said about the building of the Temple, "The people rejoiced over the offerings, for they had given freely and wholeheartedly to the Lord, and King David was filled with joy" (1 Chronicles 29:9, NLT).

DAVID DIED IN PEACE

As David came to the end of his life, he called his son Solomon aside one last time. He charged Solomon to be faithful to the Lord and His commandments, stressing this as a key to the blessing of God on the kingdom. He warned him of individuals he thought might be a threat to the security of the throne and should not, therefore, be trusted. He also advised his son of individuals who should be honored and rewarded by the new king because of the way they had treated David. It was the last opportunity David would have to advise his wise son. "So David rested with his fathers, and was buried in the City of David" (2:10).

TEN WAYS TO EXTEND YOUR FAITHFULNESS TO THE END

1. *Plan to put God at the center of everything.* David was not allowed to build the Temple because he was a man of war and bloodshed. But God allowed David to make preparations for the Temple's greatness in size, expensive gold covering; but most of all its spiritual importance. David challenged Solomon to build the Temple, "Seek the Lord your God...arise...build... bring the Ark of the Covenant into the house that is built for the Lord" (1 Chronicles 22:19, NKJV).

    When you lead a ministry—whether a class, church or educational institution—make plans for its spiritual influence in the lives of your followers. You may have many other tasks, but the most important is emphasizing the spiritual input God will have in their lives.

2. *Cast positive vision.* When David was old and preparing Solomon to take his place, he challenged his son, "The Temple...must be a magnificent structure, famous and glorious throughout the world, (1 Chronicles 22:5, NLT). Every leader will have ideas and desires for his/her ministry to continue after they depart. In the same way David cast a vision for Solomon to see in his mind a glorious and magnificent Temple. So, you as a leader will have ideas and dreams for what you want to happen in your ministry after you leave. Your followers won't know what you were planning or dreaming if you don't tell them. So then, cast a positive bright vison of what God can do through them and through the ministry.

3. *Rally support because of need.* David wanted something better after he was gone. The best way to motivate followers is to do what David did. " I am living in a beautiful cedar palace, but the Ark of God is out there in a tent" (2 Samuel 7:2). David made his point by explaining the difference between a palace and a tent. What was David doing? Rallying support to build the Temple after he was gone. Isn't that what you must do to those who follow your ministry? If you don't show them a better future that will glorify God, who will? So you will enable them to worship God better when you begin to make future plans for those following you to worship God after you are gone.

4. *Task you loved ones to a great task.* David challenged his son Solomon to, "honor the name of the Lord...God is with you... pray for wisdom...obey God...do not be afraid or lose heart" (1 Chronicles 22:11-13, NKJV). When you are a leader of God's people, make sure you connect them to God first and foremost. More than being connected to you, or to an organization, connect them to God. When your followers are connected to God and follow Him, that is the greatest compliment to your spiritual ministry.

5. *Leave directions and expectations for future successors.* "David gave Solomon the plans ... instructions how much gold to use... and a vast list of items (1 Chronicles 28:11-21). David supplied a list of the great amounts of gold, silver, plus stones, timber and building materials to be used in building the Temple. While David could not be present to supervise the construction of the Temple, he provided plans and directions for its success. When you minister to God's people today, remember their success is a credit to you. God sees what your ministry has accomplished, and even when its through your followers—God's rewards are better than any reward offered on earth.

6. *Leave directions and expectations for future success.* David gave Solomon, the plans for the Temple that were given to him by the Spirit of the Lord. He also gave instruction about gold .. list of items...and how to get everyone involved in building the Temple (1 Chronicles 28:11-21). In the same ways, you as a leader must make both preparations and give instructions how your followers will carry on the work of God when you are no longer around.

7. *Organize support.* David not only laid out the plans and blue-prints for the Temple, he gathered gold, silver, precious stones, timber and stone. But David also made perpetrations and directions for the workers. "David separated them into divisions ..." (1 Chronicles 23:6, NKJV).

The text explains how David planned occupational task, building projects, and construction goals. Even though David would not worship in the Temple, he made thorough preparations as through he would be the construction foreman, and superintendent. In the same way, as a minister for Jesus Christ you must first have a vision of the completed project, then second a vision of how it will be constructed, and third insight in the day-to-day operations, or task-by-task work to get it done.

8. *Explain the biblical rational for the task.* David's job was to plan for the building of the Temple. But what about motivation? David motivated the people to give, sacrifice and work by appealing to the ultimate reason for Christian service—it was for God's glory. "This is what the Lord has declared...'I have always moved from one place to another with a tent and a Tabernacle as my dwelling'" (1 Samuel 7:5-6, NLT). In the same way, you must always cast vision—at the beginning of the task and on a daily basis—so your followers realize the purpose for which they minister or serve.

9. *Pray for God's continual blessing.* Notice how David prayed for the construction of the Temple. "Bless the house of Your servant, that it may continue" (2 Samuel 7:29, NKJV). When you lead your people in prayer, they enter into conversation with God for the purpose of ministry. Whether they are praying for the supply of money, or the supply of material, or daily construction, or for the completion—your people must join you in intercession to God to use the ministry for them...to them...and then through them.

10. *Ask others to follow your example.* David challenged them, "Now then who will follow my example?" (1 Chronicles 29:5, NLT). When David sacrificed money for the Temple, he challenged others to follow his lead. One of the best ways to lead ministry—is to lead. Lead in sacrifice, lead in giving, lead in hard work, lead in long hours, lead in goodliness. The best quality of a leader is that followers actually follow.

AFTERTHOUGHT

WHEN did David begin seeking God? We don't know anything about his life until he was a shepherd watching over the family's sheep. So what do we know about young David—he knew about God, wanted the presence of God in his life. Very early David was a God-seeker.

David writes to describe his personal journey. "my shepherd leads me...beside still waters...makes me lie down in green pastures...leads me in right paths...and David does not fear evil walking through shadows of death.

David faced death with hundreds—or thousands watching—Goliath began to square off against David. But the 17 year old ran toward him, and with one stone from his sling, the giant fell. Then David took his sword to cut off his head. Psalm 151 tells the story of young David approaching Goliath. We don't know if Psalm 151 was actually written by David. It is found outside the inspired Bible, but it was found in the Dead Sea Scrolls.

PSALM 151

I was young among my brothers,
And the youngest in my father's house.
I tended my father's sheep.

My hands made a harp,
My fingers fashioned a lyre.
Who will tell the LORD?
The LORD Himself, it is He who hears.
It was He who sent His messengers.
And took me from my father's sheep,
And anointed me with His oil.
My brothers were handsome and tall,
But the Lord was not pleased with them.
I went out to meet the Philistines,
And he cursed me by his idols.
But I drew his own sword,
I beheaded him and took away disgrace from the people of Israel.

David spend approximately 16 years as a fugitive, running from Saul. First we see the jealousy of Saul when David killed Goliath. Remember, Saul who was present when David killed Goliath, but did not do anything. Then we saw the anger of Saul when he threw his spear at David while eating a meal. What psalm could David write.

PSALM
27:1, 5, 8-9, 14, NKJV

The Lord is my light and my salvation;
Whom shall I fear?
The Lord is the strength of my life;
Of whom shall I be afraid?
For in the time of trouble
He shall hide me in His pavilion;
In the secret place of His tabernacle
He shall hide me;
He shall set me high upon a rock.
When You said, "Seek My face,"
My heart said to You, "Your face, Lord, I will seek."
Do not hide Your face from me;
Do not turn Your servant away in anger;
You have been my help;
Do not leave me nor forsake me,
O God of my salvation.
Wait on the Lord;
Be of good courage,
And He shall strengthen your heart;
Wait, I say, on the Lord!

When David was finally crowned king—what did he do...he continued being a *God-seeker*. David wanted to focus his coronation on the Lord.

PSALM 21:1-5, NKJV

The king shall have joy in Your strength, O Lord;
  And in Your salvation how greatly shall he rejoice!
You have given him his heart's desire,
  And have not withheld the request of his lips. Selah
For You meet him with the blessings of goodness;
  You set a crown of pure gold upon his head.
He asked life from You, and You gave it to him—
  Length of days forever and ever.
His glory is great in Your salvation;
  Honor and majesty You have placed upon him.

David was a seeker of God, that does not mean he was perfect, nor does it mean he never sinned. One night when he could not sleep he walked on the roof top of his home and saw beautiful Bathsheba bathing. He was tempted and sent for her to come to his bed. David broke the 7th commandment. "Thou shall not commit adultery." He sinned against the husband Uriah, Bathsheba, and against his marriage vows. But most of all he sinned against God. But David's sin was known and the prophet Nathan pointed his conviction finger at David to announce, "Thou art the man."

Because David was a God-seeker, that sin destroyed David's walk with God. David knew it and he knew God knew it. That sin broke his fellowship-relationship with God. For a year after his sin with Bathsheba, there is no written record of any Psalm written by David. Until David's sin was known. Then he wrote Psalm 51 that reflected his broken relationship with God.

PSALM 51: 1-3, 7, 9-10, 12, 14, 17, NKJV

Have mercy upon me, O God,
  According to Your lovingkindness;
According to the multitude of Your tender mercies,
  Blot out my transgressions.
Wash me thoroughly from my iniquity,
  And cleanse me from my sin.

For I acknowledge my transgressions,
  And my sin is always before me.

Purge me with hyssop, and I shall be clean;
  Wash me, and I shall be whiter than snow.
Hide Your face from my sins,
  And blot out all my iniquities.
Create in me a clean heart, O God,
  And renew a steadfast spirit within me.
Restore to me the joy of Your salvation,
  And uphold me by Your generous Spirit.
Deliver me from the guilt of bloodshed, O God,
  The God of my salvation,
And my tongue shall sing aloud of Your righteousness.
  The sacrifices of God are a broken spirit,
A broken and a contrite heart—
  These, O God, You will not despise.

Many feel David wrote psalm 37 when he was old. David looked back over the years to testify "The wicked plot against the just...but the LORD laughs at him" (v. 12-13). David the *God-seeker* still wanted to know God and follow Him even towards the end of his life.

PSALM 37:28-29, 3-6, 16-17

For the Lord loves justice,
   And does not forsake His saints;
They are preserved forever,
   But the descendants of the wicked shall be cut off.
The righteous shall inherit the land,
   And dwell in it forever.
Trust in the Lord, and do good;
   Dwell in the land, and feed on His faithfulness.
Delight yourself also in the Lord,
   And He shall give you the desires of your heart.
Commit your way to the Lord,
   Trust also in Him,
And He shall bring it to pass.
   He shall bring forth your righteousness as the light,
And your justice as the noonday.
   A little that a righteous man has
   Is better than the riches of many wicked.
For the arms of the wicked shall be broken,
   But the Lord upholds the righteous.

At the end of David's life, he still prayed what he requested at the beginning when he was tending his father's sheep:

PSALM 23:6, NKJV

Surely goodness and mercy shall follow me
  All the days of my life;
And I will dwell in the house of the Lord
  Forever.

PART TWO

GOD SEEKER

DEVOTIONS

Week One

DAVID—FAITHFUL AS A SHEPHERD

THE following devotionals are available for pastors/teachers to email to their listeners/students. They can daily pray, read Scriptures, and apply to their life the applications of the lessons they hear in this series.

Order emails _____

Day 1	Go...Find My King
Day 2	Where Was David When He Was Found?
Day 3	Qualifications
Day 4	David—the Eighth Son
Day 5	God's Eyes
Day 6	The Spirit Moves
Day 7	David—the Best

Day 1

GO...FIND MY KING

"Now the Lord said to Samuel, 'You have mourned
long enough for Saul. I have rejected him as king
of Israel, so fill your flask with olive oil and go to
Bethlehem. Find a man named Jesse who lives there,
for I have selected one of his sons to be my king.'"

1 Samuel 16:1, NLT

HAVE you ever noticed that when a problem arises, God has a solution. The issue, we have to seek God and ask Him to help us solve our problems. One lesson to learn in your Christian life—God waits. What is God waiting for you to do? Notice the three solutions to the problem of Saul who sinned against God. First God told Samuel the prophet, "quit mourning over Saul." Does that tell us not to worry too long over one problem? Second, "fill your horn with oil." God told Samuel to get the instrument of ministry ready for use. Is God telling you to get your "instruments" ready for ministry. This could include getting mentally ready...emotionally ready...and physically ready. Are you ready for the next task God gives you?

> *Lord, I confess my sins, forgive me and cleanse me so I will*
> *be ready for ministry. Lord, I need Your Holy Spirit to flow*
> *through me, Your instrument, and then guide me into min-*
> *istry. Amen.*

The third solution God told Samuel, "Go, I am sending you" (16:1). This means action. After you pray to get ready and then you prepare to get ready—then go do it! Why? Because when God prepares His servants, He also has a task for them to do—ministry. Samuel was instructed, "go...to Jesse the Bethlehemite." Notice the promise, "I have provided." What task do you think God has prepared for you to do?

Lord, I am here waiting for You to speak to me. I will do what You want me to do. I will go where You want me to go. I will be what You want me to be. I will say what You want me to say. Amen.

READING:

1 Samuel 16:1-13;

Psalm 26

Day 2

WHERE WAS DAVID WHEN HE WAS FOUND?

*"And Samuel said to Jesse, 'Are all the young men
here?' Then he said, 'There remains yet the youngest,
and there he is, keeping the sheep.'"*

1 Samuel 16:11, NKJV

ALL seven sons lined up for Samuel. He was looking for the next king of Israel. One was missing. What was he doing? He was faithfully doing his job/task. He was not outside the door trying to get an appointment with Samuel. No! He was keeping sheep. Let's add our opinion. David was not complaining because he was not involved, nor was he goofing off because the father had overlooked him. No! David was keeping sheep. Could you say, this boy who was faithfully looking after His earthly father's sheep, will one day faithfully looking after his Heavenly Father's sheep? Does it mean that God won't call a person who is not faithfully doing their task? When God called you to salvation, what were you doing?

*Lord, I have not always been faithful to my task in life,
whether in school, at work, or otherwise. Forgive me and*

cleanse me. Teach me faithfulness in Your presence. Help me to be strong, and help me learn discipline. Amen.

God has a plan for each of us (Jeremiah 29:11), and He has a called us to our task. That doesn't mean everyone is called for fulltime Christian service. God calls or leads each of His children to their life's task. Yes, some are called to fulltime service, but not all. What has God called you to do? How has God prepared you to do the plan He has for your life?

Lord, forgive me for leaving You out of my plans for my life. Show me what You want me to do, and I will do it. Lead me to the place or task You have for my life, and I will go there. I yield myself to be Your servant and to do Your will. Amen.

READING:

Psalm 8; 21; 103

Day 3

QUALIFICATIONS

*"But the Lord said to Samuel, 'Do not look at his
appearance or at his physical stature, because I have
refused him. For the Lord does not see as man sees;
for man looks at the outward appearance, but the
Lord looks at the heart.'"*

1 Samuel 16:7, NKJV

*"But God has chosen the foolish things of the world to
put to shame the wise, and God has chosen the weak
things of the world to put to shame the things which
are mighty; and the base things of the world and the
things which are despised God has chosen, and the
things which are not, to bring to nothing the things
that are, that no flesh should glory in His presence."*

1 Corinthians 1:27-29

WHEN God chooses a person to serve Him, what is He is
looking for? First, it is not outward strength. Didn't Samson with all his strength fail the Lord? Second, its not those
with the highest IQ or highest educational standard (PhD). Remember,

Solomon was the wisest man, yet he too fail the Lord. Third, it is not earthly talent, or journalism or the ability to speak. Fourthly, it is not wealth, royal birth, or position of political or business strength. God is looking for *heart integrity*—didn't he say, "The Lord...looks at...the heart" (v. 7). So when God looked into David's heart He said, "I have found a man after My own heart" (Acts 13:22).

> *Lord, I am not perfect. I have failed You and I have sinned. Forgive me and cleanse me for service. I am not the most talented, but I surrender myself to You. Take whatever talent I have and use it to magnify Jesus Christ. I yield to be saved by You. Amen.*

David was the eighth son, but God used him. David learned the principles of life by tending sheep. David also learned how to sling a rock accurately, and God use him. David put this heart and soul into music, and God used his Psalms, and has continued to use them to this day.

> *Lord, I surrender my talents to You. With Your help I will be the best I can be in everything I do. With my heart, I yield everything to You, I will be what You want me to be, and I will do what You want me to do. Amen.*

READING:

Galatians 1:10-24;

1 Corinthians 1:18-31

Day 4

DAVID—THE EIGHTH SON

*"Thus Jesse made seven of his sons pass before
Samuel. And Samuel said to Jesse, 'The Lord has not
chosen these.' And Samuel said to Jesse, 'Are all the
young men here?' Then he said, 'There remains yet
the youngest, and there he is, keeping the sheep.'"*

1 Samuel 16:10-11, NKJV

WHEN you read the story of David, he was not even chosen to appear before the prophet Samuel. Seven sons passed before Samuel, isn't seven a perfect number? It takes seven notes to form a perfect scale. Seven colors form the perfect number in God's paint box. And there are seven days in a week. But Samuel said, "no...the Lord has not chosen these" (v. 10). David the eighth son was left out, not even asked to show up for qualifications. If seven is God's favorite number, remember, eight is God's number of a new week; the next day after Passover week. Eight is the number of *new beginnings*, and David was the new beginning of God's kingdom.

*Lord, teach me to not count the way the world counts the
seven days in a week. The eighth day is Your day. It is a new*

day and a new week. Help me look forward to new begin-
nings. Amen.

We need to remember, "The Lord does not see as man sees, for man looketh on the outward appearance, but the Lord looks at the heart" (16:7). God saw the integrity of David's heart. When did God see it? When David first looked into the heart of God, "David a man after God's own heart" (Acts 13:22). So here is a picture of David looking into God's heart, and at the same time God is looking into the young shepherd's heart.

Lord, I want to look into Your heart. I want to know You as
you really are. I will master the Bible to find out about You.
I will pray to experience Your presence. I will serve You to
allow Your power to flow though me. Amen.

READING:

Galatians 1

Samuel 16:1-13

Day 5

GOD'S EYES

"But the Lord said to Samuel, 'Do not look at his
appearance or at his physical stature, because I have
refused him. For the Lord does not see as man sees;
for man looks at the outward appearance, but the
Lord looks at the heart.'"

1 Samuel 16:7, NKJV

WHAT if you could look at people the way God looks at people? Would that make you a better supervisor at work? A better servant at church? A better parent? God looks into the heart to find that person's priorities in life. God wants to see a person's weakness or pride, lust of the flesh, or the lust of money and things. Then God looks to see a person's moral goals or aims in life. Since the first Commandment deals with the priorities of love to God and secondly love of others (Matthew 22:36-40), God wants to see how that priority works out in your life. What will God see when He evaluates your priorities and the way you make moral decisions.

Lord, I confess I am not perfect. I don't love You enough, nor
do I serve You enough. I don't love my neighbors enough, and
show them Your love. Forgive me! Cleanse me! Strengthen
me to grow and do better. Amen.

When the Lord looks into your heart, He first checks your track record. What have you done to demonstrate your love to Him...with your time...your talents...your giving. Next the Lord checks out your desires or aims in life. Do you plan to cheat on your spouse...or to steal from someone...to break His commandments? God will examine your past to get facts. Then He will exam your dreams and desires to evaluate your character.

> *Lord, I want to be a person like David—one who chose Your heart. I want to love the things You love, and I want to stay away from the things You despise. I want a heart like David's heart. I want Your heart. Amen.*

READING:

Psalm 27, 37

Day 6

THE SPIRIT MOVES

*"So as David stood there among his brothers, Samuel
took the flask of olive oil he had brought and anointed
David with the oil. And the Spirit of the Lord came
powerfully upon David from that day on. Then
Samuel returned to Ramah. Now the Spirit of the
Lord had left Saul, and the Lord sent a tormenting
spirit that filled him with depression and fear."*

1 Samuel 16:13-14, NLT

THESE two verses first give a powerful promise to what God can do when He finds a young person who not only is willing to do His will, but when he/she seeks to please the Lord (Acts 13:22). The second verse tells what began to happen to the one who not only refused to please the Lord, but denied God's presence in his life. Saul began to turn away from God, and the Spirit of God left him. David sought to please God, and the Spirit of God rested upon him. Look at your heart—are you seeking to find the heart of God as David did? Or, do you find yourself turning away from the Lord?

*Lord, You know my heart—I cannot hide from You. Forgive
my doubts and the times I have second guessed You. Give me a
pure heart that will seek Your presence and do Your will. Amen.*

Remember, both Saul (1 Samuel 10:1), and David (1 Samuel 16:13), were anointed by God to be king over God's people. However, Saul made bad choices that compounded his problem. It wasn't any one thing Saul did wrong, but many bad choices that lead to God's rejection of him as king (1 Samuel 15:35; 16:14). What about your choices in life regarding living a godly life? Or even to the point, what about your choices that directly relates to obedience to Scriptures and/or obedience to God?

Lord, forgive me for all the bad choices I have made in the past. I repent and I choose to follow You. Cleanse me and strengthen me to follow the good choices I make in the future. I want to follow You, and help me be like David in pursing Your heart. Amen.

READING:

1 Samuel 15:1-16:14

Day 7

DAVID—THE BEST

"So Saul said to his servants, 'Provide me now a man who can play well, and bring him to me.' Then one of the servants answered and said, 'Look, I have seen a son of Jesse the Bethlehemite, who is skillful in playing, a mighty man of valor, a man of war, prudent in speech, and a handsome person; and the Lord is with him.'"

1 Samuel 16:17-18, NKJV

A T this time David was about 16 years old, yet already he had a reputable resume. They were looking for someone to play the harp and sing for the king. How good was David? The Bible calls him "the sweet Psalmist of Israel" (2 Samuel 23:1). David was chosen for the top spot—to play for the king—because he qualified in many ways. His Psalms were the best and have endured for centuries. His aim was perfect to bring down Goliath. His leadership brought together twelve tribes in unity. His godly influence on the spiritual life of Israel was evident. So when man chose David, God had prepared the teen for every challenge he met. That brings the discussion to you, are you striving to be the best in everything you do? Don't measure yourself by others, what is your measurement for your improvement?

Lord, thank You for putting a good spirit in David. Thank You for his example that motivates me to do my best, and always be my best. Help me not to measure myself with others, help me see Your requirements for me. Help me to adjust my requirements to Your requirements. Amen.

There was a need for a harp player and a sweet signer. They found David and he got the position. Don't let the world determine your standard for work and living. Determine to be the best...to do the best...at all times...for all occasions.

Lord, lift my level of expectations. Don't let me do things shabby, and don't let me think second rate. Help me be my best in all I am and do. Amen.

READING:

1 Samuel 16:12-23;

Psalm 100

Week Two

DAVID—FAITHFULLY FIGHTS EVIL

THE following devotionals are available for pastors/teachers to email to their listeners/students. They can daily pray, read Scriptures, and apply to their life the applications of the lessons they hear in this series.

Order emails _____

Day 8   Focus

Day 9   Faithful to Small Responsibilities

Day 10   Wear Your Own Armor

Day 11   The Inner You

Day 12   Victory Before the Battle

Day 13   Face Your Problems

Day 14   Finish the Job

Day 8

FOCUS

*"David's oldest brother, Eliab, heard David
talking...I know about your pride and deceit.
You just want to see the battle!"*

1 Samuel 17:28, NLT

D AVID was young—16 years old—and not trained as a solider.
He was sent to bring supplies to his brothers who were fighting
the Philistines. When the teenager began asking questions, the
oldest brother accused David of false motives. Eventually David would
ask his brother, "Is there not a cause?" (1 Samuel 17:29, KJV). He could
look beyond a squabble with his brother to focus on God's reputation
and the cause of righteousness. Sometimes in life we must look beyond
our weaknesses and rise above any complaints or bickering of God's people to focus on God's reputation and God's purpose in this world.

> *Lord, forgive me for focusing on my problems and the issues
> among Christians. Help me focus my vision on You and
> the purpose You have for believers today. When I see what
> Christians should be doing, help me see my responsibility
> and do it successfully. Amen.*

Do not let other people set your agenda for your work, and ministry. Yes, there are a lot of problems, and your friends may question the

issues and challenges facing you and the church. But, ask yourself God's question, "is there not a cause?" Then focus your life and ministry on the cause God shows you.

> *Lord I cannot do everything people ask me to do, nor should I. Help me focus on Your priorities and Your needs. Help me find "your cause," then do it with purpose and accomplish that task with Your grace and strength. Amen.*

READING:

1 Samuel 17:1-58

Day 9

FAITHFUL TO SMALL RESPONSIBILITIES

"But David persisted. 'I have been taking care of my
father's sheep and goats,' he said. 'When a lion or a
bear comes to steal a lamb from the flock, I go after
it with a club and rescue the lamb from its mouth. If
the animal turns on me, I catch it by the jaw
and club it to death.'"

1 Samuel 17:34-34, NLT

A person's character usually manifests itself by the way he/she takes responsibility for the things that are put in his/her care. A person of strong character will be responsible for the things that belongs to others. David reflected an above average character when he personally faced danger and harm by not only defending his father's herds, but David went the extra mile to retrieve the lost animal He killed the predator. It is one thing to defend your own personal property, it's a greater thing to defend property that belongs to others (his father's), especially when you place yourself in danger to do it. How trustworthy are you?

Lord, teach me character and dependability. Help me see
my weaknesses, and then repent and strengthen those things

I let slip. I want people to trust me and have confidence in the words of my promises. Amen.

Not only did David protect his father's flock, he went after the predators when an animal was stolen. Note the phrase, "If the animal turns on me, I catch it by the jaw and club it to death" (1 Samuel 17:35, NLT) then David adds, "I have done this both to lions and bears" (1 Samuel 17:36, NLT). This describes both David's bravery and character.

Lord, teach me to be brave and face the dangers of life. But more than courage, teach me to always do the right things and to always trust You when I do it. Amen.

READING:

2 Samuel 22:1-51

Day 10

WEAR YOUR OWN ARMOR

"Then Saul gave David his own armor—a bronze helmet and a coat of mail. David put it on, strapped the sword over it, and took a step or two to see what it was like, for he had never worn such things before. 'I can't go in these,' he protested to Saul. 'I'm not used to them.' So David took them off again."

1 Samuel 17:38-39, NLT

YOU cannot fight the battles of life with another person's armor and sword. No, you must battle problems and sins in life with the principles that gave you past victories. You won't win spiritual battles by using another's reputation or the principles someone else uses to fight. You can learn from them, be motivated by them and ask God to help you in your struggles to give you victory, just as God has helped others to win battles. But, use the lessons that have given you victory in the past. There is strength in past victories. So be ready to battle, by the faith you learned in God's presence during your battle. Claim a new victory by new dedication and new insight from God's Word.

Lord, thank You for every lesson You have taught me, and thank You for past victories. Help me remember the steps to past victories and follow the same principles again. Amen.

You can acquire encouragement and motivations from others, but you must wear your own armor, not Saul's armor and sword. Remember what God taught you in the past, and build on that strength. Your next battle may not be won with the same answers and identical responses. But a past habit of courage and remembrance of previous victories can motivate you to learn...get strength...be courageous...and let the Lord solve the problem for and through you.

Lord, I ask for sacrificial memory to realize how You have helped me solve problems in the past. I need Your guidance to solve my present challenge. I need Your power to endure and win. I need Your help. Amen.

READING:

Ephesians 6:10-24

Day 11

THE INNER YOU

"Don't be ridiculous!' Saul replied. 'There's no way
you can fight this Philistine...you're only a boy.'"

1 Samuel 17:33, NLT

"Through God we will do valiantly,
For it is He who shall tread down our enemies."

Psalm 60:12, NKJV

YOU cannot always face life based on the opinions that others have of you. Saul put David down, "you're only a boy." Others don't always know the inner you. They may not know your strong inner self perception, nor do they know what strengths you have or how you will face a battle/problem. David may have not been strong with a sword—yet—but he was outstanding with a sling and rock. So don't let people put you down, and be careful that you don't put other people down. We never know what God can do through them.

> *Lord, thank You for inner strength from Jesus living in me.*
> *I will learn Your ways of solving problems and follow Your*
> *guidance. I will yield to Your wisdom and strength. Through*
> *Your power, I will solve problems and win victories. Amen.*

David looked beyond his strength to see God's strength. "Through God we shall do valiantly." When you identify with God, you begin to see ways to solve your problems; and when you yield to God and pray, you get strength to win victories. Let's don't be *problem focused*; let's be *God focused*. He wants to help you in your crisis, and He I will help you when you rely on Him and ask Him for help.

Lord, I face a problem/crisis. I pray for wisdom to understand my problem. Then I ask You to show me how to attack this problem and I need Your guidance to help with the various issues I face. Help me make "faith" decisions, and guide me as I work through these problems for Your glory. Amen.

READING:

Psalm 9, 17

Day 12

VICTORY BEFORE THE BATTLE

"Then said David to the Philistine, 'Thou comest to me with a sword, and with a spear, and with a shield: but I come to thee in the name of the Lord of hosts, the God of the armies of Israel, whom thou hast defied.'"

1 Samuel 17:45, KJV

"But thanks be to God, which giveth us the victory through our Lord Jesus Christ."

1 Corinthians 15:57, KJV

DAVID understood two facts that gave him victory—even before the battle began. First, David knew Goliath was armed with a spear and sword. David did not claim his strength was in his sling and rock. No! He knew victory was in God's name, i.e., "the name of the LORD of host" (v. 45). While the King James identifies "the LORD of host," the translation is the fighting army of angels. David was backed first by God, then second by a host of fighting angels. How could he lose? Then David let Goliath know the battle was not between him and Goliath, but it was God verses Goliath.

> *Lord, when I get into problems remind me I am on Your side—not the other way around. I claim Your wisdom to know what to do, I need Your strength to respond the correct way. I need Your victory to win. Amen.*

David chose five stones ...he only needed one. It was an accurate throw because he had practiced that pitch many times. But also when David claimed faith in God's victory (v. 45, 47), God guided the stone. You see God's power and David's practice working together. "David... smote the Philistine in his forehead" (v. 49). Learn a lesson in usefulness, when you have practiced a phrase of ministry and you commit it to God's control—victory will follow.

> *Lord, thank You for the illustration of David's victory. I will practice the methods and principles of ministry, so I can better trust You to give victory. Amen.*

READING:

Psalm 108,

1 Corinthians 15:54-58

Day 13

FACE YOUR PROBLEMS

*"As Goliath moved closer to attack, David quickly
ran out to meet him."*

1 Samuel 17:48, NLT

THERE are problems in life, because everything can break, run out of gas, rust out or wear out. So you cannot run from your problems, or hide from things, or ignore them. When David faced the largest problem/battle of his life, what did he do? "David ran *quickly* to meet him (v. 48). Does this give us a principles how we can face the difficulties of life? Why did David run? Because he knew God was on his side. Also, David's *faith-knew* he would win the battle. With that confidence, why wait or stand there in fear?

> *Lord, give me a "problem-solving" attitude towards life.
> Help me face future problems with confidence because I trust
> in You. Give me "faith-eyes" to look at everything in life from
> Your perspective—especially problems. Amen.*

Also, see the word *quickly*, in today's verse. David not only ran, he did it *quickly*. So when you are going to do something for God in your personal life—do it now. And if you are going to do something for God in ministry—get started *quickly*.

Lord, teach me the importance of time. Help me not to waste it, but guide me to use all of my time for Your glory. Help me work with purpose and help me not waste time, but to dedicate all my time to You, to use it for Your glory. Amen.

READING:

Psalm 27, 13, Victory Psalm 136

Day 14

FINISH THE JOB

"So David triumphed over the Philistine with only a sling and a stone, for he had no sword. Then David ran over and pulled Goliath's sword from its sheath. David used it to kill him and cut off his head."

1 Samuel 17:50-51, NLT

A S soon as the stone knocked Goliath to the ground, David ran over to finish the job. Three lessons! First, a job is well done, when a job is finished, so David wanted complete victory. Second, the enemy did not know if the stone killed Goliath, but when David held up the head of Goliath the enemy had a change of heart—they fled. Third, with David holding the head, the soldiers were given courage. Whereas before, no one would fight Goliath because they were afraid of the Philistine army. Then "the men of Israel...rushed after the Philistines, chasing them" (v. 52). Let's learn lessons from David to always work for victory and complete the task. Also, remember, your faithfulness will motivate others to be faithful in service.

> *Lord, thank You for the example of David. May I be faithful in every task I have to do. Give me inner discipline to be a "finisher" in the tasks I have in life. Also may I be a positive testimony to my family and friends. Amen.*

Some might think that David was a typical teenager who was showing off when he took the head to Jerusalem (v. 54). Was David telling the inhabitants I will capture Jerusalem one day? Then that night, they "brought him to Saul with the Philistine's head still in his hand" (v. 57). Up until that victory, it was the greatest event in David's life, and thereafter victory over Goliath became a symbol of David's victorious life.

Lord, thank You for the examples of victory in David's life. Help me to learn from David ,and may the principles of David's victory be a guide in my life. Help me be victorious and keep me trusting You for all victories. Amen.

READING:

1 Samuel 17:48-58;

Psalm 109

Week Three

DAVID—FAITHFULLY WRITING PSALMS TO GOD

T HE following devotionals are available for pastors/teachers to email to their listeners/students. They can daily pray, read Scriptures, and apply to their life the applications of the lessons they hear in this series.

Order emails _____

Day 15   David Hungered After God

Day 16   Pray the Psalms

Day 17   Psalms of Deep Feelings

Day 18   The Future

Day 19   Prayer for Wisdom

Day 20   Psalms When You Sin

Day 21   Psalms of Worship

Day 15

DAVID HUNGERED AFTER GOD

*"One thing I have desired of the Lord, that will I
seek: that I may dwell in the house of the Lord all the
days of my life, to behold the beauty of the Lord, and
to inquire in His temple. For in the time of trouble
He shall hide me in His pavilion; in the secret place
of His tabernacle He shall hide me;
He shall set me high upon a rock."*

Psalm 27:4-5, NKJV

PEOPLE think David's strength was in his military victories, such as defeating Goliath. Others think his strength was his wise rule to unite the tribes into one nation and govern them successfully. Those were contributing factors, but David's strength was his God who gave him victory and wisdom. And David's unseen source was his continual reliance on God and hunger to know God more and serve Him better. David said, "one thing I have desired," summarizes the essence of David's reason for living, and David's key to success.

*Lord, give me David's passion to know You. I identify with
David's "one desire" to fellowship with God in His house. I*

want to experience the beauty of the Lord as David found
fulfillment in Your perfection. Amen.

You must pray with David, "teach me Your ways, O Lord, and lead me in a smooth path" (Psalm 27:11, NKJV). God will answer that prayer when you obey the rest of the Psalm, "Wait on the Lord...He shall strengthen your heart. Wait, I say, on the Lord!" (27:14, NKJV). Just as David found the answer to the challenges of life in God's presence, so your answer to your life's problems is found in God's presence.

Lord, David pursued Your heart and found it. I will fol-
low his example. I will purse Your presence. I need wisdom...
teach me. I need guidance...lead me. I need strength...give
me courage. I need assurance... show me Yourself. Amen.

READING:

Psalm 27; 42

Day 16

PRAY THE PSALMS

"The heavens declare the glory of God;
and the firmament shows His handiwork."

Psalm 19:1, NKJV

"In the night His song shall be with me."

Psalm 42:8, NKJV

SOME Psalms challenge you to action, others remind you of God's goodness, and still others are imprecatory Psalms where you pray judgment on evil workers and your enemies. But many Psalms are prayers. You can pray the words of a Psalm to God, just as David talked to God through songs and poetry. So pray God's greatness, "The heavens declare the glory of You my God, I see Your handiwork in the earth" (Psalm 19:1, AMP). When God gives you great insight, or helps you solve a problem pray, "lead me in the right paths according to Your name, as I walk through the valley of shadows about death" (Psalm 23:3-4).

> *Lord, You are the wisdom I need, teach me. You have the road map of life, guide me. You have living waters, satisfy my thirst. You have the bread of life, I am hungry. Amen.*

Sometimes the Psalms are not about your hurts and needs. They focus on God, giving praise and glory to Him. "Come before His presence with singing...enter into His gates with thanksgiving" (Psalm 100:2, 4). Why? "The Lord is good, His mercy is everlasting, and His truth endures to all generations" (Psalm 100:5).

Lord, forgive my stumbling words. I will praise You with Psalm. "To You O Lord, I sing praises" (Psalm 101:1). "Bless the Lord, O my soul, and all that is within me, bless His Holy name" (Psalm 103:1). Amen.

READING:

Psalm 19, 100, 101, 103

Day 17

PSALMS OF DEEP FEELINGS

"As the deer longs for streams of water, so I long for you, O God. I thirst for God, the living God. When can I go and stand before him? Why am I discouraged? Why is my heart so sad? I will put my hope in God! I will praise him again—my Savior and my God!"

Psalm 42:1-2, 11, NLT

YOU pray the Psalms because they express the deep anxiety of your heart when it is hard to put your feelings into words. The Psalmist was being tormented by accusations. He was like a young deer being chased through the forest by wild hungry dogs that would eat him up. The deer didn't know if he could keep running away from his predators. All he needed was a refreshing drink of water. In the cool of a stream the deer could drink cool water to get strength to out-run the dogs. Have you ever been pursued by threats that would kill you? Stop in the presence of God, drink His water. He will give you strength to out-run your attackers.

Lord, I pause in Your presence for peace of mind. Give me Your favor and show me my path through my problems. I need water and direction. Ah! Water is good! Amen.

Jesus said, "If anyone thirst, let him come to Me and drink. He who believers in Me...out of his heart shall flow rivers of living waters" (John 8:37-38, NKJV). Just as the deer needed water, so David when he was pursed by Saul who wanted to kill him, needed spiritual and physical rest. That same rest is available to you today.

Lord, I will stop to find Your presence. I am walking through the valley of the shadow of death, and I need Your assurance. Then You say to me, "I will be with you. Come walk with Me to find refreshing waters. Then walk with Me through the valley." Amen.

READING:

Psalm 42; 23

Day 18

THE FUTURE

"The Lord said to my Lord, 'Sit in the place of honor
at my right hand until I humble your enemies,
making them a footstool under your feet.'"

Psalm 110:1, NLT

"For the Lord declares, 'I have placed my chosen king
on the throne in Jerusalem, on my holy mountain.'"

Psalm 2:6, NLT

WE look through the eyes of David to see the future ruling King of Israel. It is not Solomon, look further into the future—into our future. David had prophetic eyes to see the Messiah sitting over Israel's future. The Son of David who will sit on the future throne is Jesus Christ. David saw and heard the LORD Jehovah saying to the LORD of David—Jesus Christ—to sit on David's throne. That will happen at Jesus' Second Coming. Then Jesus will sit on the throne to judge the enemies of God, "make Your enemies Your footstool" (Psalm 110:1). So, when you sing Psalm 2 and 110, you are praying to the Lord Jesus Christ who will one day rule from David's throne.

Lord, I come to You asking for mercy and forgiveness of my sins. I cannot rejoice in Your punishment of evil men when I know I am not perfect. Forgive me by the blood of Calvary. I stand before You in Your perfect righteousness that You have imputed to me. Amen.

How could David know so much about Jesus Christ? David lived approximately 1,000 years before Jesus was born in Bethlehem. The Spirit of God gave David prophetic eyes to see the future (2 Samuel 7:4-29). Also, David had faith that God's kingdom was greater than any earthy kingdom. And that one day God would rule the world through His Son of David, i.e., the Lord Jesus Christ.

Lord, thank You for rewarding Your servant David with eyes to see the future. Remove my spiritual blindness when I read Your Word. Help me to understand the "days" in which I live, and guide me as I prepare for the future. Amen.

READING:

Psalm 2, 110

Day 19

PRAYER FOR WISDOM

"Take delight in the Lord, and He will
give you your heart's desires."

Psalm 37:4, NLT

"Open my eyes to see the wonderful
truths in your instructions."

Psalm 119:18, NLT

D AVID had the deep assurance of God's guidance, "You guide me with your counsel, leading me to a glorious destiny" (Psalm 73:24, NLT). He prayed for this assurance based on the Word of God. "Open my eyes to see the wonderful truths you have for me" (Psalm 119:18, NLT). A close examination of David's prayers revel his constant dependence on God to direct his life. David revealed that dependence in his constant prayer for God to guide and direct his life. How dependent are you in God's guidance of your life? How often do you ask God to guide the daily details of your life? Create a list of verses to constantly pray for daily guidance.

Lord, open my spiritual eyes to see Your hand in my life.
Guide me through the details of this day. Help me plan for

a better tomorrow, based on what You teach me today and what I am learning from You. Amen.

David had a "God consciousness" as he lived each day. Do you have a consciousness of God's indwelling presence as you move through you daily life? Remember, Jesus Christ lives in your body (Galatians 2:20; Philippians 1:20). Christ lives in you whether you are in church, or at the market place. He indwells you as you pray even if you forget about your Christian standards to doubt or even deny Him. Since Jesus lives in your heart, call out to Him in trouble...in difficulties...in failure...and in good times. You can always ask Him to help you.

Lord, remind me to call out to You, even when I forget. Remind me to ask for help even when I am solving problems. Hear me when I praise You for the good things in my life. Lord I need You now, listen to me and answer. Amen.

READING:

Psalm 37:1-40;

Psalm 119:1-24

Day 20

PSALMS WHEN YOU SIN

"Wash me clean from my guilt. Purify me from my sin. Against You, and You alone, have I sinned; I have done what is evil in Your sight. You will be proved right in what You say, and Your judgment against me is just. Purify me from my sins, and I will be clean; wash me, and I will be whiter than snow."

Psalm 51:2, 4, 7, NLT

EVERYONE needs to pray the Psalm of repentance, for all have sinned. Some sins seem more evil than others in our sight, but all sins are the same to God. All sins block our access to God, so we need to cry out in repentance and ask for forgiveness. David's sin was great, reminding us that some sins have greater human consequences than other sins. David committed adultery with another man's wife, then arranged for the husband—Uriah—to be killed in battle. Today, that is called murder two—manslaughter. Just as David had to enter God's presence to beg for forgiveness and cleansing, so you might need to seek God's presence to ask for forgiveness and to be cleansed. We have God's promise, "If we confess our sins, He is faithful and just to forgive... and cleanse...of all unrighteousness" (1 John 1:9).

Lord, I have sinned knowingly, forgive me, and cleanse me. Also, I have sinned ignorantly (Psalm 19:12-13), and I never have live the perfect godly life. Forgive and cleanse me. Amen.

Because of David's godly life and spiritual attainment, his sin was even more terrible than anything else. Yet the greatness of David's previous walk with God did not make any allowances for God's reaction to David's sin. God feels the same about David's sin and your sin. So, pray the words David found in Psalm 51:

Lord, "create in me a clean heart...restore to me the joy of Your salvation" (Psalm 51:10-11). Help me learn from my repentance, to never go there again. Help me keep my eyes on Jesus. Keep my heart pure and my eyes on Jesus. Amen.

READING:

Psalm 51

Day 21

PSALMS OF WORSHIP

"O Lord, our Lord, Your majestic name fills the earth! Your glory is higher than the heavens."

Psalm 8:1, NLT

"I will exalt You, Lord, for You rescued me. You refused to let my enemies triumph over me. Sing to the Lord, all you godly ones! Praise His Holy name."

Psalm 30:1, 4, NLT

THE Psalms are filled with praise and thanksgiving to God for all He did for David. David always praised the Lord as he rose from being a shepherd, to being a warrior, to being a king ruling all God's people. David praised God just as excitedly when the family overlooked him as the youngest son and shepherd, and when he ruled all the tribes, and all God's people. Can you praise God on bad days, and as well as the good days? Can you give thanks when someone is trying to destroy your reputation or finances, as you do when you have a great success? Make praise a habit of your conversation with God. Tell the Lord how thankful you are for all the good things in your life.

Lord, I stop to thank You for what I have learned from my failures yesterday—last week. I praise You for Your help in the good things I accomplished yesterday—last week. Help me keep my eyes on You in the good days as well as bad days. May I glorify You in my successes and failures. Amen.

David had a lot of bad days. Saul tried to kill him for several years, and when David had a chance to kill Saul—he honored the Lord (1 Samuel 24:6, 10). In David's "good" years and "hard" years, he always trusted in the Lord. From his youth, David composed and sang Psalms to the God. We have him doing the same in his last days (2 Samuel 23:1-7; 2 Chronicles 29:10-20).

Lord, give me a joyful heart to praise You for all You are doing for me. Give me a grateful heart to thank You for all You have done for me. I worship You, for You alone deserve our praise and thanksgiving. Amen.

READING:

Psalm 8, Psalm 30:1-12

Week Four

DAVID—FAITHFULLY TO GOD'S CALLING

THE following devotionals are available for pastors/teachers to email to their listeners/students. They can daily pray, read Scriptures, and apply to their life the applications of the lessons they hear in this series.

Order emails _____

<table>
<tr><td>Day 22</td><td>Jealousy Began It All</td></tr>
<tr><td>Day 23</td><td>David the Fugitive</td></tr>
<tr><td>Day 24</td><td>How Long in the Wilderness</td></tr>
<tr><td>Day 25</td><td>The Patience of Faith</td></tr>
<tr><td>Day 26</td><td>More Patience of Faith</td></tr>
<tr><td>Day 27</td><td>What to Do When God Does Not Answer</td></tr>
<tr><td>Day 28</td><td>God Replaced Saul with David</td></tr>
</table>

Day 22

JEALOUSY BEGAN IT ALL

"This was their song: 'Saul has killed his thousands, and David his ten thousands!' This made Saul very angry. 'What's this?' he said. 'They credit David with ten thousands and me with only thousands. Next they'll be making him their king!' So from that time on Saul kept a jealous eye on David."

1 Samuel 18:7-9, NLT

SATAN can use any sin to destroy a person, and he will. In the same way satan will use anything to destroy the work of God, and he used jealousy to turn Saul against David. At the beginning, "Saul eyed David" (v. 9), but with time Saul's jealousy grew into hatred. This grew into a murderous rage. Over the next 12 years Saul did everything he could to kill David. Rather than chasing the enemies of Israel, Saul chased David. This was just a small thing. On one occasion Saul rallied over 3,000 men to hunt David down. Think of the loss of man hours that could have been used to built up and fortified Israel...or helped build walls for protection. Don't let jealousy or hatred in your life destroy the good things you could do for God, but not only what you could do positively for God; don't let hatred ruin your goal.

Lord, help me keep my eyes on Jesus and serve as He served. Keep me pure within and protect me from jealousy and hatred of anyone—whether saved or unsaved. Give me a love for You that influences my love for others. Amen.

Saul began with all the optimistic challenge a man had to serve God. It wasn't one thing that got Saul off track, it was several things. Each one moved him a little farther from God, each one ruining his personal character. Watch your self—both in big temptations and little sins that can destroy your life. It is sad, that David's positive deeds for God were viewed with skeptical eyes by Saul.

Lord, keep my eyes on Jesus, help me look at the world through Jesus' eyes and help me project salvation to them. Help me see needy believers through Jesus eyes, and show me how to help them. Show me my weaknesses through Jesus' eyes, and led me to strengthen my faith and obey Your Words. Amen.

READING:

1 Samuel 18:1-16; 19:1-18; 22:1-5

DAVID THE FUGITIVE

*"So David escaped and went to Ramah
to see Samuel, and he told him all
that Saul had done to him."*

1 Samuel 19:18, NLT

*"David, 'What have I done?' he exclaimed. 'What
is my crime? How have I offended (Saul) your father
that he is so determined to kill me?'"*

1 Samuel 20:1, NLT

GOD was with David the shepherd, and He was with David the champion. Now for the next several years, God will be with David the fugitive. David will not be safe at home in Bethlehem, nor any place near the headquarters of Saul. Today's Scripture readings expresses the innocence of David. His life was threatened, and he had done nothing. It's amazing how God uses the forces of evil and satan to strengthen His followers. In his late teens and twenties, David will not sit on the throne of Israel. Saul will be there, but God had Samuel anoint David as the next king. What will David learn as a fugitive, that he couldn't have learned anywhere else? David will learn faithfulness as he pursues the heart of God (Acts 13:22). David will learn how God protects...God provides...and God guides. The greatest lesson of all—David will learn to know God.

Lord, teach me the lessons You taught David. Thank You I don't have the difficulties of David, but still; I want to experience the lessons David learned as he was a man after Your own heart. Amen.

God prepares us for our life's callings in different ways. God used sheep to teach David how to lead people. What will God use to teach you to serve Him? God used Goliath to teach David how to fight evil, how will God teach you to stand strong? God used David's years as a fugitive to teach him about the Lord's protection. Have you learned that lesson?

Lord, thank You for teaching David Your protection as he was chased by Saul to kill him. Teach me Your protection of my life—show me the many ways You do it. Thank You for Your faithfulness to me. Help me be faithful to You. Amen.

READING:

Psalm 13; 34;
1 Samuel 19:18-42

Day 24

HOW LONG IN THE WILDERNESS

"Come with great power, O God, and rescue me!
Defend me with Your might. Listen to my prayer,
O God. Pay attention to my plea. For strangers are
attacking me; violent people are trying to kill me.
They care nothing for God."

Psalm 54:1-3, NLT

THERE were many who told Saul where David was hiding. Doeg the Edomite told Saul that David had gone to Ahimelech (1 Samuel 21:21 ff). What was David's reaction to Doeg, "All day long you plot destruction, your tongue cuts like a sharp razor" (Psalm 52:2). Then the Ziphites told Saul, "We know where David is hiding" (1 Samuel 23:19). Again, what was David's reaction? "Come with great power, O God, and rescue me!...strangers are attacking me, violent men are trying to kill me" (Psalm 54:1, 3, NLT). Can you image hiding for 12 years with someone searching to find and kill you? David learned to trust God Who was stronger than his enemies. He learned security in God's presence. "For you have rescued me from my troubles, and helped me to triumph over my enemies" (Psalm 54:7, NLT).

Lord, remind me of Your watch care for me, when I didn't realize I was in danger. Thank You for Your protection when I didn't realize I needed protection. Help me learn Your protection from David's life. I thank You and praise You for Your watch care. Amen.

David's years of wondering and hiding from Saul as a fugitive was a trying time. Yet during those pressure experiences David wrote many of his Psalms about threats...dangers...betrayal...trials, etc. Imagine the frustration in Saul because he could not catch David. But also, imagine the confidence in David knowing one day he would be king and reign over God's people.

Lord, teach me to go through hard days as David was triumphant over difficulties. Help me see my life's plan for my future and trust in You. Give me the faith that David had, so I can also be victorious. Amen.

READING:

Psalm 54; 56;

1 Samuel 21:1-9; 22:1-23

Day 25

THE PATIENCE
OF FAITH

*"He said to his men, 'The Lord forbid that I should
do this to my lord the king. I shouldn't attack the
Lord's anointed one, for the Lord Himself has chosen
him.' So David restrained his men and
did not let them kill Saul."*

1 Samuel 24:6-7, NLT

DAVID'S companions wanted him to kill Saul while he had the opportunity. Saul had come into the cave at En-gedi to relieve himself. David and his men were hiding in the back of the cave. David's men tried to persuade David, "now's your opportunity" (1 Samuel 24:4, NLT). But David did not look at circumstances to make him king. He did not listen to the crowd. David was pursuing God's heart (Acts 13:22), therefore David was doing what God wanted him to do. If you had an opportunity for advancement in business or elsewhere—but you had to lie...cheat...or step on someone else to do it—would you do it? Everyone will be tested concerning their character and honesty, ask God to give you victory when the opportunity comes.

*Lord, teach me to keep my eyes on You as I walk, live, and
serve You in this life. Lead me to make the right decisions to*

follow You and always make the "right" decision. Keep me
faithful to You. Amen.

David didn't rationalize that God had anointed him king. No!
Also, David didn't look at his terrible circumstance, again; No! Also,
David didn't give into the pressure of his companions, nor did he exer-
cise youthful impatience. None of that. David looked pasted his crown
and he looked past the kingdom. David was looking for the heart of
God. "God said, 'I have found David...a man after my own heart'" (Acts
13:22).

Lord, give me Your eyes to see me as You see me. Give me
spiritual eyes to see what the Holy Spirit wants to do in my
life. Give me future eyes to see what You want to do with my
life. Then help me do it. Amen.

READING:

1 Samuel 24: 1-22;

Psalm 57

Day 26

MORE PATIENCE
OF FAITH

"He [David] *sent out spies to verify the report of
Saul's arrival. So David took the spear and jug
of water that were near Saul's head. Then he and
Abishai got away without anyone seeing them or
even waking up, because the Lord had
put Saul's men into a deep sleep.*

1 Samuel 26:4, 12, NLT

DAVID silently crept into Saul's camp. God had protected David by putting Saul and his guards into a deep sleep. Again David had an opportunity to kill Saul, but again did not do it. David expressed faith to his companions, "Surely the Lord will strike Saul down someday, or he will die of old age or in battle" (1 Samuel 26:10, NLT). All David took was Saul's spear and jug of water. Isn't that ironic? Was this the spear that Saul hurled at David to kill him in the palace (1 Samuel 19:10)? And didn't Saul use his sword to kill himself (1 Samuel 31:4)? Why did David take his spear? It was Saul's chief defense. But also, it demonstrated that even a person's best defenses are not enough. Only God can protect us.

*Lord, thank You for the patience of David. He did not try to
"kill" his way into the rulership of God's people. Thank You*

for his faith. Teach me to patiently trust You for the things in life. Help me look beyond circumstance to Your plan and Your way. Amen.

This is the second time David sneaks into Saul's camp and has an opportunity to kill Saul. That should show the patience of God to Saul, but apparently it didn't. Saul continued in his evil ways. But it also says something about David. The future king did not plan to enter office this way. David was a man of faith. He trusted God to give him the kingdom. It was approximately 15 years from the time Samuel anointed David king until he finally became ruler of God's people. Then it was only one tribe. David had to wait an additional seven years to rule all twelve tribes of Israel.

Lord, teach me the patience of David. Forgive me for running ahead of Your timing. Give me the faith of David to do Your work...in Your way...at Your time. Give me the vision of David to purse Your heart (Acts 13:22). Amen.

READING:

1 Samuel 26:1-25;

Psalm 11

Day 27

WHAT TO DO WHEN GOD DOES NOT ANSWER

"And when Saul inquired of the Lord, the Lord did not answer him, either by dreams or by Urim or by the prophets."

1 Samuel 28:6, NKJV

THERE came a time when God didn't answer the petitions of king Saul. Even though God put Saul into office, the Lord deals with us in the *now*. And when is that? "Now is the accepted time" (2 Corinthians 6:2, NKJV). Saul had compromised too many times. His jealousy to kill David had controlled his life too many times. That, plus many other times Saul had displeased the Lord. "The Lord did not answer him." There are many reasons why God does not hear your prayers. The obvious is sin in your life (John 9:31). Also, God does not hear if you doubt His ability to answer, or you doubt His presence (Mathew 21:20). Also, don't ask for the wrong reasons, and don't ask God to do something He cannot do.

Lord, Saul could not pray or communicate with You because of too many compromises or sins in his life. I confess my sins, forgive me, and cleanse me (1 John 1:9). Put me on praying

*ground to fellowship with You so I can pray to receive an-
swers. Amen.*

Saul had hit the bottom when God refused to answer him or communicate with him. If you have sin in your life—like Saul—there are steps
to reach the heart of God. First repent of all known sin and promise
never to return. Then ask God to forgive you by the blood of Christ (1
John 1:7). Confess your sins—calling them by name (1 John 1:9). Jesus
Christ will hear and forgive (1 John 2:1-2).

*Lord, I come to You with requests upon my heart. But first
I confess my sins and ask for the blood of Christ to cleanse
them. I will learn to pray, teach me patience in praying; then
faith in prayer, and finally teach me persistence in praying.
Amen.*

READING:

1 Samuel 28:1-25;

1 John 1:1-2; 2

Day 28

GOD REPLACED
SAUL WITH DAVID

"And when He had removed him, He raised up for
them David as king, to whom also He gave testimony
and said, 'I have found David the son of Jesse,
a man after My own heart, who will do all My will.'"

Acts 13:22, NKJV

IF ever there was a man with great potential to do great things for God—it was Saul. Outwardly he had all the qualification, but inwardly he lacked character. What is that? Character is habitually doing the right thing in the right way at the right time, for the right purpose. Saul failed at almost every point. But David qualified simply with one statement. "God said...David...a man after My own heart" (Acts 13:22, NLT). David wasn't perfect, and David displeased God on several occasions. But when David chased the heart of God...what did he find? David found the presence of God. David knew God intimately, and in his Psalms, David talked with God, David praised God and worshiped God.

> *Lord, thank You for Your patience with Saul, but even more*
> *thank You for patiently preparing David to build Your king-*
> *dom greater than any other could do. Help me learn from*
> *David, and lead me to do all I can do for Your glory. Amen.*

What else did David find in the heart of God? "David found favor with God" (Acts 7:46, NLT). And what is favor, it is a special priority to those who earn it. How did David earn God's favor? He asked to please the Lord, "This also will please the Lord, more than sacrificing animals" (Psalm 69:31, NLT). David's heart was right, and God put all things together for him to rule the kingdom.

Lord, I want to please You in all I think and do, just as David pleased You. I want Your favor, just as David found favor from You. Hear the prayers of my heart and favor me. Amen.

READING:

Psalm 69:1-36

Week Five

DAVID—FAITHFULLY AS A NEW KING

THE following devotionals are available for pastors/teachers to email to their listeners/students. They can daily pray, read Scriptures, and apply to their life the applications of the lessons they hear in this series.

Order emails _____

Day 29   Waiting to Move Up

Day 30   Only Half the Kingdom

Day 31   Unity at Last

Day 32   Committed to Doing Right

Day 33   Dreams of Jerusalem

Day 34   New Attack

Day 35   Right Thing...Wrong Way

Day 29

WAITING TO MOVE UP

"David inquired of the LORD, saying, 'Shall I go up to any of the cities of Judah?' And the LORD said to him, 'Go up.' David said, 'Where shall I go up?' And He said, 'To Hebron.'"

2 Samuel 2:1, NKJV

NOTICE three things, first David was on "talking-terms" with God. Since David had talked to God on a continual basis, he asked about becoming king. Second, David sought God's permission. Saul was dead, and he had been anointed as future king. But still David asked permission. Third, David asked for direction. He asked the "where" question. God answered "Hebron." Since God knew the future for David, He led David to the "spiritual" center of the tribe of Judah. Those were the people who would recognize David as king. When you need direction concerning a decision, follow the example of David in seeking direction from God.

> *God, I will come to You first when I face big decisions. Then I will ask You if I should take certain actions, or go in certain ways. Finally, I will ask for specific directions. I will let You led and guide my life. Amen.*

Even though David had been anointed king over the people by God, he still prayed about moving forward. Even though Saul was dead, and the people needed leadership, David still prayed about making a decision and moving to a new place. Then David didn't wait for the people to come seek him, David went to Hebron. Will you follow these three steps when facing big decision/moves in your life?

Lord, forgive me when I have moved too slow in the past seeking Your direction. Also, forgive me for the times I have run ahead to quickly. Teach me patience...I am waiting on You. Amen.

READING:

2 Samuel 2:1—2:4

Day 30

ONLY HALF THE KINGDOM

"The men of Judah came and there they anointed David king over the house of Judah...Abner... commander of Saul's army took Ishbosheth the son of Saul...made him king over Gilead...over all Israel."

2 Samuel 2:4, 8-9 NKJV

DAVID was anointed by God over all the tribes of Israel. Saul had kept David from the throne for fourteen years Now the son of Saul—Ishbosheth—will keep the ten northern tribes for another seven years. Imagine the disappointment to David, yet he faithfully served the Lord with his ministry to God's people. Did David regret not killing Saul when he had the chance to grasp the whole kingdom? No! David faithfully led Judah. Why? Because when David sought the heart of God, he found the faithfulness of God, and David determined to live that example—David was faithful in this smaller sphere of rulership.

Lord, teach me the patience of David. When I cannot do everything, help me faithfully accomplish what You have given me to do. When other people get things I think I need, or I want; teach me patience. Lord, help me live faithfully over small things, so I will be qualified for greater responsibilities. Amen.

The ten northern tribes were led by Saul's son. On the surface it looked like a good division of labor over God's people. But there were many tensions...skirmishes...and outright wars. Also, there was trickery by some who tried to put the twelve tribes back together. David remained faithful to God and waited. If you wanted something as big as the ten tribes taken from David, would you be patient? Would you remain faithful?

Lord, teach me patience long before I desperately need it, so I will trust You in any future pressure situations. Lord, teach me faithfulness as You taught it to David. Amen.

READING:

2 Samuel 2:1-3:1

Day 31

UNITY AT LAST

"Then all the tribes of Israel came to David at Hebron...saying, 'Indeed we are your bone and your flesh'...therefore all the elders came ... and David made a covenant with them...before the Lord. And they anointed David king over Israel."

2 Samuel 3:1, 3, NKJV

APPROXIMATELY twenty years earlier David had been anointed king over God's people. Many events happened in those twenty years, but finally God's people are untied. The elders recognized the physical unity, "we are your bone and your flesh" (v. 1). Now David would give the military unity to defend the people against attack. David would give the spiritual unity; the Ark was brought to Jerusalem. David would give them political unity; they would be one nation - one people—one future. When all the tribes came together, they could do many things together under David's leadership, they could never do separately.

> *Lord, I love unity with You, we are one. Give me unity in my family to grow together spiritually. Give me unity in my church to worship You together as one body. Give me unity with my friends to minister together for Your glory. Amen.*

When the twelve tribes came together in unity to crown David king, that was not the end. Not at all. That was the beginning of God's evidential movement in the nation. Attacking enemy nations were defeated. Jerusalem was captured and made the capital. The Ark of the Covenant (God's presence) was brought to Jerusalem. Other surrounding nations were beaten and paid tribute to Israel. Yes, unity was a wonderful spirit because it brought a glorious future.

Lord, teach me the lessons of unity. Help me overlook the faults of others and live in harmony with them. Help me strengthen them, as I wait for them to strengthen me. I want unity for more than a good feeling—I want unity for expanded ministry and more glory to You. Amen.

READING:

2 Samuel 5:1-25;

Psalm 125; 126; 133

Day 32

COMMITTED TO DOING RIGHT

"In the past, when Saul was our king, you were the one who really led the forces of Israel. And the Lord told you, 'You will be the shepherd of My people Israel. You will be Israel's leader.'"

2 Samuel 5:2, NLT

NOTICE the two things the leaders of all the tribes said to David when they crowned him king. First, they reminded David that he was the one who really defended the people. While Saul was chasing David and attending to his own agenda, David and his men were actually the defenders of the nation. That meant, David protected God's position over the nation and defended law, order and the worship of God. When David spent all those years running from Saul; both God and the people saw his honesty. They counted David as their leader. What does God and "the people" see about you? Are you a defender of God's priority?

> *Lord, I will be honest before You. Help others see my commitment to truth and doing right. Then use me to testify to Your "law and order." May I be an effective witness for You. Amen.*

There was a second thing. The leaders remembered God had ordained David to be the spiritual leader of God's people, i.e., "you will be shepherd of My people Israel" (v. 2). News of David's anointing as king by Samuel apparently spread far and wide. The people knew about it; now David's coronation was taking place. Can you rely on the promises of God taking place, just as the people of Israel?

Lord, You had a plan for David's life and his anointing told the people. I know You have a plan for my life. May my life, and actions, and words verify Your work in my life. Thank You for calling me...for choosing me...for using me. Amen.

READING:

2 Samuel 5:1-4;

1 Chronicles 11:1-3;

Psalm 78 (Israel's history to David)

Day 33

DREAMS OF JERUSALEM

"David then led his men to Jerusalem to fight against the Jebusites, the original inhabitants."

2 Samuel 5:6, NLT

"David said, 'Whoever is first...will become the commander of my armies!' And Joab was first."

1 Chronicles 11:6, NLT

"Whoever attacks them should strike by going into the city through the water tunnel."

2 Samuel 5:8, NLT

THE first vision of the newly crowned David was to capture the fortress of Jerusalem. It was the symbolic center of the enemy's grip on the Holy Land. It was David's dream location for his capital. As a young shepherd, David led his sheep to drink the clear water from the Pool of Siloam. There he learned about a tunnel/canal thought solid rock from the top of Mount Zion, so inhabitants could draw fresh water (there is no other natural water in Jerusalem). So, Joab climbed up this long well into the city. There, Joab snuck his fellow warriors into Jerusalem, and they captured the city.

Lord, thank You for helping David formulate a strategy to capture Jerusalem and that city has been "Your" city throughout history. Thank You for preparing many "things" throughout history for me to enter Your "city of salvation" to serve You. Amen.

David was a shepherd in the field, surrounding Bethlehem and Jerusalem. He learned things in his youth that helped him become a conqueror in his adult life. Help me remember the things You have done for me in my youth; then help me use them in my adult life.

Lord, thank You for memory. I praise You for the lessons I learned as a youth that help me in my present life. I will build on what You have taught me, and serve You today. Keep teaching me new lessons to serve You better in the future. Amen.

READING:

2 Samuel 5:6-25;

1 Chronicles 11:4-25

Day 34

NEW ATTACK

*"When the Philistines heard that David had been
anointed king of Israel, they mobilized all their
forces to capture him. But David was told they were
coming, so he went into the stronghold."*

2 Samuel 5:17, NLT

WHEN David became king of God's people, the first to
attack him were the Philistines. After all, the Philistines,
had not been defeated by king Saul. So they thought
David was just the next king. They expected to keep the "little nation of
Israel" bound up and on the defensive. But David was not just another
king, and he was nothing like Saul. God was working through David.
So, when the Philistines attacked David they didn't expect a counter
attack. David prayed, "should I go out to fight the Philistines?" (v. 19).
God answered "yes" (v. 19). David not only defeated them, "they (the
Philistines) abandoned their idols there" (v. 21). Both God and David
were victorious.

> *Lord, I love following You and I am not naive—I know sa-
> tan will attack me. I will be strong, and I will follow You.
> Give me wisdom to not only "stop" evil in my life, but give me
> strength to prevail and march triumphantly for You. Amen.*

Notice the first thing David did when attacked, "David asked the Lord" (v. 19). Make prayer your constant defense against temptation and attacks of evil. Pray with Jesus, "Deliver me from the evil one" (Matthew 6:13, MVP). As the new king of Israel, David not only had to defend the nation from attacks, David had to go on the offensive to take back land that was originally "God's land."

Lord, I pray against evil influences in my life. May I live a holy life that brings glory to You. But I also pray against the evil one who is the source of temptations to destroy me. Give me victory over the evil one. Amen.

READING:

2 Samuel 5:17-25;

Matthew 6:7-18

Day 35

RIGHT THING...
WRONG WAY

*"Then David again gathered all the elite troops
in Israel, 30,000 in all. He led them to Baalah of
Judah to bring back the Ark of God, which bears
the name of the Lord of Heaven's Armies, who
is enthroned between the cherubim. They placed
the Ark of God on a new cart and brought it from
Abinadab's house, which was on a hill. Uzzah and
Ahio, Abinadab's sons, were guiding the cart."*

2 Samuel 6:1-3, NLT

WHEN David became the new king, one of the first positive things he did was to capture Jerusalem and make it God's city The next positive step was to focus God's people on the LORD and bring the Ark of the Covenant back to Jerusalem. At first, David did it the human way, i.e., "placed the Ark of God on a new cart" (v. 3). It was commendable they used a "new" cart, but God's plan originally was for the Ark to be carried on the shoulders of the Levitis (Numbers 4:15). When the oxen stumbled, man's attempt to steady the Ark brought God's judgment. Since God is so exact about "holy things" make sure you stay pure in things relating to God.

Lord, David wanted to do the right thing, but he did it in the wrong way. Teach me to always do the right things Your way. Keep me from doing "dumb" things in my own way. Amen.

David had the correct response to God's judgment." David was now afraid of the Lord" (v. 9). Then David obeyed God and had the Ark brought to Jerusalem on the shoulders of the Levites. With every six steps, David "sacrificed a bull and a fattened calf" (v. 13). Now the steps of the priest were "covered" by a "blood sacrifice." Remember, "without shedding of blood there is no remission" (Hebrews 9:22).

Lord, thank You that David could learn after their human mistake. Thank You for the blood sacrifice that brought Your presence in the Ark into Jerusalem. Thank You for the sacrifice of Jesus that brings Your presence into my life. Amen.

READING:

2 Samuel 6:1-19;

Hebrews 9:1-24

Week Six

DAVID—FAITHFUL TO REPENT AFTER TERRIBLE SIN

THE following devotionals are available for pastors/teachers to email to their listeners/students. They can daily pray, read Scriptures, and apply to their life the applications of the lessons they hear in this series.

Order emails _____

Day 36   David's Sin

Day 37   Thou Art the Man

Day 38   God's Mercy

Day 39   David Prayed and Fasted

Day 40   What Repentance Looks Like

Day 41   Repentance Leads to Victory

Day 42   David's Thanks for Peace

Day 36

DAVID'S SIN

*"In the spring of the year, when kings normally go
out to war, David sent Joab and the Israelite army to
fight the Ammonites. They destroyed the Ammonite
army and laid siege to the city of Rabbah. However,
David stayed behind in Jerusalem."*

2 Samuel 11:1, NLT

SOMETIMES we get in trouble for what we don't do, not for the
things we do. David didn't go fight Israel's enemies, he sent Joab
and "all Israel." That phrase probably meant not only soldiers, but
support and supply groups. Technically everyone was there except David
their leader. How bad is this, read 2 Samuel 8, "David attacked the Philistines" (v. 1), "David defeated Hadadezer" (v. 3), "David killed twen-
ty-two thousand" (v. 5), "David took ..." (v. 7), "David made himself
a name...killing eighteen thousand Edomites" (v. 13). The name David
and victory were synonymous. As long as David led Israel, they were
victorious. Did he get overconfident and stayed home? Be careful when
you are ministering the work of God that you don't get overconfident
and leave ministry to someone else.

*Lord, thank You for the positive examples of David and his
victories. May I have victories in my personal life. May I never get overconfident and give up my ministry to You. Amen.*

The story of David's sin with Bathsheba is well known. God's response, "The thing that David had done displeased the Lord" (2 Samuel 11:27). Not only did Uriah die in battle, but David's sin scarred his testimony...the child died...all as a result of David's first problem—not going to battle. But then the ultimate curse of David's problem was his sin with Bathsheba.

Lord, help me be vigilant in serving You and may I never seek ease for the sake of ease. May I work at ministry when there is a task to perform. Yes, I will take a "Sabbath rest" that You provide, but I will work when there is work to do. Amen.

READING:

2 Samuel 11:1-27

Day 37

THOU ART THE MAN

"The rich man owned a great many sheep and cattle.
The poor man owned nothing but one little lamb...he
raised...grew up with his children...cuddled it in his
arms...a guest arrived at the home of the rich man
...took the poor man's lamb...killed it...
prepared it for his guest."

2 Samuel 12:1-4, NLT

DAVID thought he "covered" his sin against Uriah, until Nathan the prophet told the above parable to David. Remember, David had been a shepherd, so, "David was furious" (v. 5). He vowed, "the man...deserves to die" (v. 5). David demanded the man pay fourfold, i.e., "four lambs" (v. 6). At this point, Nathan pointed his finger at David, "Thou art the man" (v. 7). God used this parable/story to convict David of his great sin. David repented of his great sin, and begged God for forgiveness (Psalm 51). Yet there were consequences for this flagrant sin.

Lord, forgive me when I have swept my sins under the carpet
as David. I repent of my sin...forgive me...cleanse me...restore
me to Your fellowship...cleanse me...use me to serve You. Amen.

Just as David demanded a "four-fold" payment for sin, there was a four-fold consequences for David's sin. First, the child from the adulterous affair died. Second, David's daughter Tamar was raped. Third, David's son Aamon was murdered. And fourthly, David's son Absalom died in rebellion to his father. Yes, David grieved over his sin because it broke his relationship with God. But still, David grieved over the four consequences of his sin.

Lord, forgive all my sins, those things I remember and repent of them. Forgive any sin I did ignorantly or sin I have forgotten. Forgive me and restore my fellowship with You. Amen.

READING:

2 Samuel 12:1-25;

Psalm 51

Day 38

GOD'S MERCY

*"Then David comforted Bathsheba his wife, and
went in to her and lay with her. So she bore a son,
and he called his name Solomon. Now the Lord
loved him, and He sent word by the hand of Nathan
the prophet: So he called his name Jedidiah,
beloved of the Lord."*

2 Samuel 12:24-25, NLT

L ET'S look at two pictures of God. First, God is holy who judges sin, "Our God is a devouring fire" (Hebrews 12:29, NLT). On the other side, God is merciful and kind, He is a forgiving God. Yes, God allowed the child conceived in adultery to die (2 Samuel 12:19). But following that event, God gave to David and Bathsheba a son— Solomon. Solomon would take over the kingdom and extend David's ministry. God could have given David a son by another wife to take over the kingdom. But No! God used Bathsheba to continue the line, and remember, she and David were in the line of Messiah—Jesus Christ (Matthew 1:6). When you think of your sin—praise God for forgiving you, and then using you after He restores you.

*Lord, thank You for forgiving my sin and not punishing
me as You could have. Thank You for Your amazing grace.
Thank You that You used me again after I repented and*

begged Your forgiveness. I love Your mercy and I enjoy Your grace. Amen.

Since David's sin with Bathsheba was well known (Psalm 51), God used this experience as an example of His mercy and goodness. So testify, "His goodness and mercy shall follow me all the days of my life (Psalm 23:6, NKJV). Just as God had a plan for Solomon to build the Temple, and write three books in the Old Testament, God has a plan for your life after you "mess up." But examine David's life...his repentance... his worship...and his pursuit of God's heart. Then ask for God's favor.

Lord, I have sinned, and I am sorry. Forgive me. Teach me Your grace and help me walk in Your mercy. Show me Your favor and use me in Your ministry. Amen.

READING:

2 Samuel 12:24-25;

1 Chronicles 22:5-19;

Psalm 90

Day 39

DAVID PRAYED AND FASTED

"He went without food and lay all night on the bare ground."

2 Samuel 12:16, NLT

"I fasted and wept while the child was alive...but why should I fast when he is dead?...I will go to him one day, but he cannot return to me."

2 Samuel 12:22-23, NLT

PRAYER and fasting can move the heart of God to answer a request. But God did not hear the prayer of David to let the child live. However, David's fasting and prayer indicated his true repentance for his sin. While fasting did not save the child, it changed David. He learned true repentance. "Against You, and You alone have I sinned" (Psalm 51:4, NLT). David also leaned true restoration, "Restore to me the joy of Your salvation ... then I will teach Your ways to sinners" (Psalm 51:12-13). David's prayer after his sin revealed both aspects of "David...a man after my heart." David pursed God's heart in honest worship, but also in honest repentance.

Lord, forgive me for not pursuing Your heart in good times and after I have sinned. Teach me sincerity. May I worship You in good times, but also, may I worship You when I repent, and You forgive me. Amen.

Immediately when David heard the child had died, "he went to the Tabernacle and worshiped the LORD" (v. 20). Just as David wholeheartedly pursed the LORD for the life of the child, then when he learned the child was dead, he wholeheartedly pursed the LORD in worship. What better way to live...wholeheartedly fast about problems...wholeheartedly worship because God sits on the throne. Even when He sits on the throne of judgment of sin.

God, teach me to fast and prayer with all my heart about my problem. But also teach me to worship with all my heart when I don't get the answers I seek. Amen.

READING:

2 Samuel 12:1-25;

Matthew 6:16-18

Day 40

WHAT REPENTANCE LOOKS LIKE

"David pleaded with God...David lay all night on the ground...David rose up from the ground...went to the house of the Lord and worshiped."

2 Samuel 12:16, 20, NKJV

L ET'S look at David to see what repentance and forgiveness looks like. First, David pleaded. Can you hear them tell God, "My sin is always before You" (Psalm 51:3). Next listen to David as he lays prostrate on the ground before God, "Against You, You only, have I sinned" (Psalm 51:4). His sin was not primarily against Uriah the husband, or against the child who died, or against the people and the Word of God he was commissioned to lead. No, David's sin was against God, so David was at the right place. God's presence, saying the right thing "wash me thoroughly from my iniquity" (Psalm 51:2). With the right heart attitude, "wash me and I shall be whiter than snow" (Psalm 51:7). Have you ever repented that deeply from your sins against God?

Lord, forgive me when I did not honestly face my sins and repent. Cleanse me from all sin—ignorant sins and careless sins—wash me white as snow. I want to stand pure before You. I want to worship You in integrity. Amen.

When David said, "purge me" (v. 7), he was asking for "sin-cleansing." Have you ever experienced the renewed spirit of a "new heart" (v. 10)? When David asked for a "new heart," it was not the old one made better, it was Holy Spirit created, so the Spirit of God (v, 12) would give him the joy of salvation.

Lord, I pray for a "sin-cleaning" of my heart. I want You to wash it as clean as a new heart. I want to stand before You clean and pure. Thank You for spiritual renewing. Amen.

READING:

2 Samuel 12:13-23;

Psalm 51

Day 41

REPENTANCE LEADS
TO VICTORY

*"So David gathered the rest of the army and went to
Rabbah, and he fought against it and captured it."*

2 Samuel 12:29

THE problem began when David didn't go with his army to
fight against Rabbah, capital of Ammon. This tribe had always
opposed God's people and terrorized them. So David launched a
war against them, but sent his army without him. Israel had always been
successful when David fought with them. David's sinned with Bathsheba
while on furlough. We had examined David's repentance, now let's look
at what he did after getting right with God. David rejoined his army and
captured the city of Rabbah, then subdued them. "Then David and all
the army returned to Jerusalem" (v. 31). So when you deal with your sin
and get victory over it, then is the opportunity to go back to doing what
you previously did for God...and obviously more.

> *Lord, thank You for the example of David's complete confes-
> sion and repentance (Psalm 51). I will follow David's exam-
> ple to completely confess all my sin and I will repent and claim
> victory in my life. Remind me that the battle against sin is
> Your battle, not mine. I will let You give me victory. Amen.*

"Then David went to Rabbah and removed the crown from the king's head, (a) and it was placed on his own head. The crown was made of gold and set with gems, and he found that it weighed seventy-five pounds. (b) David took a vast amount of plunder from the city. (c) He also made slaves of the people of Rabbah and forced them to labor with saws, iron picks, and iron axes. (1 Chronicles 20:2-3, NLT). The Bible described a complete victory, that is what you want over evil in your life.

Lord, I am weak, but You are strong enough to give me complete victory over sin. I surrender to Your authority and power. "I can do all things through Christ who strengthens me" (Philippians 4:13). Amen.

READING:

2 Samuel 12:26-31;

1 Chronicles 20:1-8;

1 Corinthians 15:51-58

Day 42

DAVID'S THANKS
FOR PEACE

*"I was glad...let us go into the house of the LORD...
standing inside your gates...to give thanks to the
name of the LORD...may there be peace within
your walls and prosperity in your palaces."*

Psalm 122:1-2, 4, 7, NLT

AVID'S Psalm praised God after he returned to the peace and
security of Jerusalem and destroyed the heathen gods in the
city of Rabbah. He felt the presence of God when he returned
to the fortification of the City of David. He enjoyed the triumphant
victory given by God. He enjoyed the protection of his home city. But
perhaps most of all, David enjoyed the opportunity "to give thanks to
the name of the LORD" (v. 4). If you are defeated by sin or burdened
with the cares of this world, look to God in repentance and rejoice in the
victory He gives. Then enter the security of the presence of God, enjoy
Him, and stop to worship.

> *Lord, remind me there is a celebration of worships on the
> other side of repentance and restoration. Help me look be-
> yond my problems and sin to see You waiting to rejoice with
> me in victory. Amen.*

Did you see the love David had for Jerusalem in Psalms 122? It was not stone and timber. No! David looked back to the memories of what God had done for him in the past, in the streets, and the palaces, and the temple. Primarily David rejoiced in God and what He did in Jerusalem. Can you look beyond failure and disappointment to expect God meeting you with His presence? Why not seek him now.

Lord, I come seeking nothing more than You—to enjoy Your presence—to worship You and rest in Your peace. The world is a topsy-turvy place, and I want to enjoy Your presence. Amen.

READING:

Psalm 122; 133; 136

Week Seven

DAVID—FAITHFUL AT THE END

T HE following devotionals are available for pastors/teachers to email to their listeners/students. They can daily pray, read Scriptures, and apply to their life the applications of the lessons they hear in this series.

Order emails _____

Day 43   Who Will Take David's Place

Day 44   That Which Cost Me Nothing

Day 45   God-Seeking

Day 46   David Thinks About the Future

Day 47   Your Body a Temple

Day 48   David's Example

Day 49   Be a God-Seeker

Day 43

WHO WILL TAKE DAVID'S PLACE

"About that time David's son Adonijah, whose
mother was Haggith, began boasting,
'I will make myself king.'"

1 Kings 1:5, NLT

"Bathsheba went into the king's bedroom. He was
old...'My lord you made a vow...your son Solomon
will surely be the next king.'"

1 Kings 1:15, 17, NLT

WHEN David was about to die, his son Adonijah decided, "I will make myself king" (v. 5). Adonijah gathered prominent leaders under David—Joab and Abiathar to sacrifice to God, anoint him king and sponsor a banquet to celebrate his new office. Did you see "Adonijah appointed himself." Also, he did not invite those close to David, or Solomon. When Bathsheba heard she told David, who was not too old to go into action David followed God's plan to anoint a king. First Zadok the priest anointed Solomon. Next David said, "Solomon is to ride on my mule" the official mule for king's transportation. Next blow the trumpets to announce, "God save the king." Then have the priest anoint Solomon into the office. Finally, the official act—Solomon sat on David's throne.

Lord, in Adonijah's self-glory, he took things to himself. May I always put You first in my life. May I always do the right thing, in the right way, at the right time—for Your glory. Amen.

All the people responded to Solomon, "God save king Solomon." While this was not a democratic government, the multitude recognized that Solomon had ascended to the throne in a public way that was orderly and followed biblical ways. Adonijah and his group were having a banquet, when they heard the trumpets and shouts of the people for Solomon. The friends left Adonijah. They realized they were on the "wrong side" and it was not God's side. Then Solomon became king and there was peace.

Lord, thank You for this insight into David handling a problem in the right way. Help me handle problems in Your way...the right way...for the right purpose...and all for Your glory. Amen.

READING:

1 Kings 1:1-2:35

Day 44

THAT WHICH COST ME NOTHING

"Then the angel of the Lord told Gad to instruct David to go up and build an altar to the Lord on the threshing floor of Araunah the Jebusite."

1 Chronicles 21:18, NLT

"Then David said, 'This will be the location for the Temple of the Lord God and the place of the altar for Israel's burnt offerings!'"

1 Chronicles 22:1, NLT

AVID was warned not to take a censes of God's people (21:3), but did it anyway. Isn't David like a lot of us who don't listen. We like David do what we want. "God was displeased with the census" (21:9). God gave David three choices for punishment. "So the Lord sent a plague upon Israel" (21:14). The angel of the Lord that brought the plague approached Jerusalem. Then David confessed his obstinance, and the angle stopped at the threshing floor of Araunah (next to Jerusalem). It was there David went for a sacrifice. Araunah tried to give the piece of ground to David—free. Listen to David's response, "I will not take that which is thine for the Lord...David gave six hundred shekels of gold...and David built there an altar" (1 Chronicles 21:24-25).

> *Lord, I will sacrifice my money for Your ministry, just as David. I don't want to offer to You "that which cost me nothing." Your son Jesus gave all for me, I want to give Him my whole life and I will worship with tithes and more. Amen.*

The spot was the future location for Solomon's temple, right next to the historic city of Jerusalem. Eventually the wall of the city took in the temple.

> *Lord, history speaks to me, telling me where You did a great work, when the Spirit of God came on Your people. I have been to the Temple Mount in Jerusalem. In the future, I will visit that spot with You after the rapture. I also want to go back to Calvary with You. Amen.*

READING:

1 Chronicles 21:1-22

Day 45

GOD-SEEKING

"Now seek the Lord your God with all your heart and soul. Build the sanctuary of the Lord God so that you can bring the Ark of the Lord's Covenant and the holy vessels of God into the Temple built to honor the Lord's name."

1 Chronicles 22:19, NLT

DAVID was a God-Seeker, when he was older he challenged Solomon and the national leaders to join him, "seek the Lord your God will all your heart" (v. 19). Even when David was a young shepherd, God was the focus of his life. "The Lord is my Shepherd" (Psalm 23:10. In his first major conflict with Goliath, God was the focus of his victory. As a fugitive David hid out in the wilderness, but he was not alone, God was David's passion, "one thing have I desired of the LORD, that will I seek after, to dwell in the house of the LORD all the days of my life." Are you a God-seeker? Do you seek God to understand Him? Or do you seek God because you love Him and want to spend time with Him?

> *Lord, forgive all my sins so nothing blocks me from seeking You. I want to know You—to talk with You—to enjoy Your presence—to worship You for saving me. Amen.*

David had a picture of God looking over the balcony of heaven, searching for anyone who was sincerely seeking Him. "The Lord looked down from heaven...if anyone truly...seeks God" (Psalm 14:2, NLT). Should God look in your direction today, would He see you seeking Him? God was pleased with David because David was a God-seeker.

Lord, I want to be a God-seeker. Forgive me for letting other things become so important in my life, that I give You second place in my thinking. I repent—I will seek You with my whole heart. Amen.

READING:

1 Chronicles 22:6-19;

Psalm 27, 42

Day 46

DAVID THINKS ABOUT THE FUTURE

*"David settled in his palace...rest from all the
surrounding enemies...David said...but the Ark of
God is out there in a tent...this is what the Lord has
declared...he will make a house for you, a dynasty
of kings! For when you die...your own offspring...his
kingdom strong...your kingdom will continue
for all time...forever."*

2 Samuel 7:1-2, 5, 11, 16, NLT

BEFORE David was an old man, God spoke to him through Nathan the prophet. David wanted to build a house for God—the most commendable undertaking in David's life. But God said to David, I will build "your house," not an earthly dwelling. God will work through the life of David for a son to be born who will do all the earthly things David desired—plus all the additional benefits that only Jesus Christ will do. God is giving David a promise that the earthly king could only begin to imagine. This son of David would usher in eternal peace and prosperity to all those who have the faith of David—i.e., David's faith in God.

*Lord, I look back to see Your promises to David. Thank You
for including David in Your planning. Thank You these*

promises apply to me. One day in the future Jesus Christ will reign and I will have perfect peace, security-eternally and happiness greater that anything I experienced on earth. Amen.

Remember, David was a man who pursed God's heart. So when David began to think about his future, God had already thought about David's future. He was living in a city that would be called "City of David" (Matthew 1:1). Because David put God first in his life, God was planning an exciting future for the earthly king.

Lord, teach me to pursue Your heart as David pursed You heart. I want to walk in communion with You as did David. Amen.

READING:

2 Samuel 7:1-29;

1 Chronicles 17:1-27

Day 47

YOUR BODY A TEMPLE

"I have worked hard to provide materials for building the Temple of the Lord—nearly 4,000 tons of gold, 40,000 tons of silver, and so much iron and bronze that it cannot be weighed. I have also gathered timber and stone for the walls, though you may need to add more. You have a large number of skilled stonemasons and carpenters and craftsmen of every kind. You have expert goldsmiths and silversmiths and workers of bronze and iron. Now begin the work, and may the Lord be with you!"

1 Chronicles 22:14-16, NLT

DAVID wasn't allowed to build the temple because he was a man of war who spilt much blood (1 Chronicles 28:3). But David did everything he could to gather all the materials needed for a human house worthy of the LORD. David gathered gold, silver, bronze, timber, and stone. Not only that, he gathered craftsmen to assemble the Temple—the most magnificent Temple that the best workers of that day could construct. Now, your body is a temple for God. Paul says, "Know ye not that ye are the temple of God" (1 Corinthians 3:16). Just as God came to live in Solomon's Temple, so the Spirit of God lives in your body. Make sure His testimony shines from your life.

*Lord, I want You to come live in my body. I will not put
anything that is sinful in my body. I will not compromise my
body. I want to glorify You with my body, Just as You were
glorified by Solomon's Temple. Amen.*

"The priest carried the Ark of the Covenant into the inner sanctuary
of the Temple the most Holy Place...a thick cloud filled the Temple of
the LORD...for the glorious presence of the LORD filled the Temple (1
King 8:8, 10-11, NLT). What a complete picture of God filling Solomon's Temple. He will do the same for you. Wouldn't it be wonderful to
experience the presence of the LORD in your human temple?

*Lord, I confess all my sins—cleanse me—fill me with Your
presence. Just as Your dwelled in Solomon's Temple, I want
You to come dwell in the temple of my body. I yield it to you.
Amen.*

READING:

1 Kings 8:1-66

Day 48

DAVID'S EXAMPLE

*"Then King David turned to the entire assembly and
said, 'now then who will follow my example.'"*

1 Chronicles 29:1, 5, NLT

WHAT better challenge could David give at the end of his
life...follow my example. After all a leader has to lead in
every area of his life. He must lead in vision-setting. David
had a dual vision, to build Israel into a strong nation and to seek God's
presence and worship Him in His house/tent. But a leader also leads
by example. He leads into battle...he leads people into the Tabernacle
to worship...he leads in godliness...he leads in following the Lord. Ask
yourself, are you a strong leader? Where is your strength? How can you
strengthen those who work with you?

> *Lord, You are my leader and example. I want to be godly
> ... I want to be serving others...I want to be Your worshiper.
> Use my example to encourage others. Forgive my mistakes
> and help me strengthen my weaknesses. I want to be a godly
> leader to point others to You. Amen.*

Notice what happened when the people followed David's leadership.
"David was filled with joy" (1 Chronicles 29:9). If you will be a godly
leader like David then you will rejoice. But it doesn't end there. "Then

David praised the Lord in the presence of the whole assembly" (v. 10). David was not a closet Christian. While that is a good place to begin meeting God. When others recognize you are a *God-seeker*, then you must give all credit and praise to God.

> *Lord, thank You for working in my heart to call me to follow You. I will be faithful, and I will serve You to the best of my ability. Lord, I don't do it for people's praise, I do it for Your glory. Amen.*

READING:

1 Chronicles 29:9-29;

Luke 9:23-62

Day 49

BE A GOD-SEEKER

*"And Solomon, my son, learn to know the God of
your ancestors intimately. Worship and serve him
with your whole heart and a willing mind. For the
Lord sees every heart and knows every plan and
thought. If you seek him, you will find him. But if
you forsake him, he will reject you forever."*

1 Chronicles 28:9, NLT

DAVID gave Solomon the challenge of being king in front of
"all the officials of Israel" (v. 1). This included religious leaders,
generals and captains of the army, overseers of the palace and
"all the others" (v. 1). David challenged Solomon with three challenges.
First, "know the God of your ancestors intimately" (v. 9). Don't miss the
word "intimately." Second, "worship and serve (God) with all your heart
and willing mind" (v. 9). That means not holding back anything—no
secrets from God. Third, "seek Him and you will find Him" (v. 9). This
book calls David a *God-seeker*, which is the secret of David's success. So,
seek God for success in your life.

> *Lord, I want You to favor my life as You favored David's life
> (Acts 7:46, NLT). I will study Scriptures and the history of
> Your Christian leaders to learn and live the principles of suc-*

cess. I will worship You with my whole heart. I will become a
"God-seeker" so You can favor me with Your presence. Amen.

David had one warning in the last challenge. "If you forsake Him He will reject you"(v. 9). Don't forsake God in big ways and never before others. But also don't forsake God in small ways—those private places in your heart. For our great God is everywhere present, including knowing your thoughts and desires. Don't forsake Him in your private world.

Lord, thank You for saving me...teaching me...keeping me...
and guarding me. I will not forsake You publicly or private-
ly. Amen.

READING:

1 Chronicles 29:1-21;

1 Kings 2:1-10

PART THREE

GOD SEEKER

LESSONS

Lesson Introduction:

ANSWER KEY

DAVID FOUND FAITHFULNESS IN GOD'S HEART

INTRODUCTION

1. David the eighth son of Jesse (1 Samuel 16:10-11). Eight – new **beginnings**.

2. God rejected Saul. "The LORD said...'I have rejected him (Saul)... fill your horn with oil...go'" (1 Samuel 16:1).

3. **Qualification**: "The Lord seeth not as man seeth, man looketh on the outward appearance, but the Lord looketh on the heart" (1 Samuel 16:7, KJV). "God...said, 'I have found David...a man after My own heart'" (Acts 13:22).

CHAPTER 1:
DAVID—FAITHFUL AS A **YOUNG SHEPHERD**

"I kept my father's sheep...came a lion, and a bear, and took a lamb...I went after...I caught him by his beard and smote him" (1

Samuel 17:34-35). *He learned, "The Lord is my Shepherd, I shall not want"* (Psalm 23:1).

CHAPTER 2:
DAVID—FAITHFULLY <u>FIGHTS EVIL</u>:
1 SAMUEL 17:1-58

Not David's battle, but God was challenged. "Is there not a cause" (17:29). *"He hast defied the armies of the Living God"* (v. 36). *"I come ... in the name of the LORD of Host...whom thou has defied"* (v. 45). *"David prevailed over the Philistine with a sling and a stone"* (v. 50).

CHAPTER 3:
DAVID—FAITHFUL <u>WRITING PSALMS</u> TO GOD

David learn to read, write, and memorize Scriptures to fulfill the Old Testament command. "Observe to do according to all the law which Moses...commanded you...meditate on it day and night that you may observe it according to all that is written in it...for the Lord your God is with you wherever you go" (Joshua 1:7-9).

CHAPTER 4:
DAVID—FAITHFUL TO GOD'S CALLING:
1 SAMUEL 26:1-5

Saul chased David with 3,000 men to kill him (26:2). "David came by night...Saul lay sleeping...his spear stuck in the ground... the Lord forbid that I should stretch out my hand against the Lord's anointed" (26:9-11). "David took the spear...cried to Abner...you are worthy to die" (26:12-16).

CHAPTER 5:
DAVID—FAITHFUL AS A NEW KING

"The Lord said to David...'go up to Hebron there they (Judah) anointed David king'" (2 Samuel 2:1-4). "Come all the tribes of Israel to David...anointed David king" (2 Samuel 5:1-3). He made Jerusalem the capital and brought the Ark of the Covenant to the city.

CHAPTER 6:
DAVID—FAITHFUL TO
REPENT AFTER TERRIBLE SIN

"David sent Joab...to battle...David stayed in Jerusalem...he saw a woman washing...took her...lay with her...conceived...'I am with child'" (2 Samuel 11:1-5). David sent husband to her, he refused. Told Joab to put Uriah in fieriest battle and retreat. He was killed, David guilty. David married Bathsheba and child was born. Parable, "thou art the man" (12:7). Daivd fasted but the child died (Psalm 51).

CHAPTER 7:
DAVID—FAITHFUL <u>AT THE END</u>

*Bought threshing floor to build altar (<u>**future Temple site**</u>). "I will surely buy it ... offered burnt offering to the LORD" (2 Samuel 24:23). When Adonijah tried to make himself king, David from his sick bed, determined and* <u>**planned Solomon's coronation.**</u>

Solomon...shall reign after me" (1 Kings 1:30). God told Daivd, "Thou shalt not build me a house to dwell in" (1 Chronicles 17:4). Before his death, David **prepared** *money, materials, stone, gold, silver, nails, and timber to build the Temple (1 Chronicles 22:14-19).*

SEVEN LESSON IN COMING SERIES

1. Ten ways to <u>**prepare**</u> to be a faithful leader.

2. Ten steps to <u>**fight**</u> evil.

3. Ten ways to find God's <u>**presence**</u>.

4. How to fulfill <u>**life's calling**</u>.

5. How to enter a new position/job.

6. Ten steps to <u>**restoration**</u>.

7. Ten steps to <u>**extend**</u> your faithfulness after you are gone.

DAVID FOUND FAITHFULNESS IN GOD'S HEART

INTRODUCTION

1. David the eighth son of Jesse (1 Samuel 16:10-11).
   Eight – new _____ .

2. God rejected Saul. "The LORD said...'I have rejected him (Saul)...
   fill your horn with oil...go'" (1 Samuel 16:1).

3. _____ : "The Lord seeth not as man seeth, man
   looketh on the outward appearance, but the Lord looketh on the
   heart" (1 Samuel 16:7, KJV). "God...said, 'I have found David...a
   man after My own heart'" (Acts 13:22).

CHAPTER 1:
DAVID—FAITHFUL AS A _____

*"I kept my father's sheep...came a lion, and a bear, and took a
lamb...I went after...I caught him by his beard and smote him"* (1

Samuel 17:34-35). *He learned, "The Lord is my Shepherd, I shall not want"* (Psalm 23:1).

CHAPTER 2:
DAVID—FAITHFULLY _____:
1 SAMUEL 17:1-58

Not David's battle, but God was challenged. "Is there not a cause" (17:29). *"He hast defied the armies of the Living God"* (v. 36). *"I come ... in the name of the LORD of Host...whom thou has defied"* (v. 45). *"David prevailed over the Philistine with a sling and a stone"* (v. 50).

CHAPTER 3:
DAVID—FAITHFUL _____ TO GOD

David learn to read, write, and memorize Scriptures to fulfill the Old Testament command. "Observe to do according to all the law which Moses...commanded you...meditate on it day and night that you may observe it according to all that is written in it...for the Lord your God is with you wherever you go" (Joshua 1:7-9).

CHAPTER 4:
DAVID FAITHFUL TO _____:
1 SAMUEL 26:1-5

Saul chased David with 3,000 men to kill him (26:2). "David came by night...Saul lay sleeping...his spear stuck in the ground... the Lord forbid that I should stretch out my hand against the Lord's anointed" (26:9-11). "David took the spear...cried to Abner...you are worthy to die" (26:12-16).

CHAPTER 5:
DAVID—FAITHFUL AS A _____

"The Lord said to David...'go up to Hebron there they (Judah) anointed David king'" (2 Samuel 2:1-4). "Come all the tribes of Israel to David...anointed David king" (2 Samuel 5:1-3). He made Jerusalem the capital and brought the Ark of the Covenant to the city.

CHAPTER 6:
DAVID—FAITHFUL TO
_____

"David sent Joab...to battle...David stayed in Jerusalem...he saw a woman washing...took her...lay with her...conceived...'I am with child'" (2 Samuel 11:1-5). David sent husband to her, he refused. Told Joab to put Uriah in fieriest battle and retreat. He was killed, David guilty. David married Bathsheba and child was born. Parable, "thou art the man" (12:7). Daivd fasted but the child died (Psalm 51).

CHAPTER 7:
DAVID—FAITHFUL _____

Bought threshing floor to build altar (_____). "I will surely buy it ... offered burnt offering to the LORD" (2 Samuel 24:23). *When Adonijah tried to make himself king, David from his sick bed, determined and _____ .*

Solomon...shall reign after me" (1 Kings 1:30). *God told Daivd, "Thou shalt not build me a house to dwell in"* (1 Chronicles 17:4). *Before his death, David _____ money, materials, stone, gold, silver, nails, and timber to build the Temple* (1 Chronicles 22:14-19).

SEVEN LESSON IN COMING SERIES

1. Ten ways to _____ to be a faithful leader.

2. Ten steps to _____ evil.

3. Ten ways to find God's _____ .

4. How to fulfill _____ .

5. How to enter a new position/job.

6. Ten steps to _____ .

7. Ten steps to _____ your faithfulness after you are gone.

DAVID—FAITHFUL AS A YOUNG SHEPHERD

A. DAVID—FIRST NOTICED:
1 SAMUEL 16:1

1. <u>First</u> noticed by God. "How long will you mourn for Saul…I have provided Myself a king (among the sons of Jesse)" (1 Samuel 16:1).

2. <u>Standard</u>. "I…see not as man sees…outward appearance … I look at the heart" (16:7).

3. <u>Eighth chosen</u>. "Seven…sons passed before Samuel…the Lord has not chosen them (16:10).

4. David <u>faithful in daily task</u>. "He is keeping the sheep" (16:11).

5. David faithful in music skills. Recommended to king because he was "a skillful player of the harp" (16:16), and "can play well" (v. 17).

6. Refreshed the king. "David…played it (harp)…refreshed and well" (v. 21).

7. Daivd faithful to his sheep. "A lion, and a bear...took a lamb ... I went after it...caught it by its beard...killed it" (17:34-35).

B. DAVID—THE LORD HIS EXAMPLE/GOAL IN LIFE: PSALM 23

1. David wrote as a young sphered, "The Lord is my Shepherd" (v. 1):

   a. Primary protector.

   b. **Personal**.

   c. **Present tense**.

2. The Lord was David's **provider**:

   a. "I shall not want."

   b. "Lied...green pastures."

   c. "Still waters."

   d. "A table of food."

   e. "Full cup."

3. The Lord **guided** Daivd. "Lead me in right paths" (v. 3).

4. **Protected** in danger. "Walk thought the valley of the shadow of death" (v. 4). Three comforting ideas:

   a. **Through**.

   b. **Shadow**.

   c. **With me**.

5. To keep Daivd on course (v. 4):

   a. Rod – **correction**.

   b. Staff – to **protect or lift up**.

6. Three sources of strength (v. 5):

   a. **Table** of food.

   b. Anoint head.

   c. Cup **overflowing**.

7. Two watch dogs to watch over sheep and David (v. 6).

   a. Goodness of God to **overwhelm**.

   b. Mercy, to **forgive and restore**.

8. Three conclusions:

   a. Because the Lord was David's Shepherd, **I shall not want** (v. 1).

   b. Because the Lord was with him, **I will fear no evil** (v. 4).

   c. Because of the Lord's loving kindness, **I will dwell in the His house** (v. 6).

C. TEN WAYS TO PREPARE TO BE GOD'S LEADER

1. **Love** the work/ministry God has given you.

2. **Identify** so the work/ministry becomes you, and you are it.

3. **Presence** locate yourself with your work/ministry.

4. **Represent** yourself with your work/ministry, i.e., Daivd as shepherd.

5. **Protect** what God has given you.

6. **Feel** with the successes/failures of your work/ministry.

7. **Serve** faithfully your work/ministry.

8. **Associate** with the success/failures, and reward/loss of work/ministry.

9. **Support** work/ministry totally.

10. **Enjoy** the rewards of work/ministry, i.e., meals, anoint head, God's house.

Lesson 1:

DAVID—FAITHFUL AS A YOUNG SHEPHERD

A. DAVID—FIRST NOTICED: 1 SAMUEL 16:1

1. _____ noticed by God. "How long will you mourn for Saul...I have provided Myself a king (among the sons of Jesse)" (1 Samuel 16:1).

2. _____ . "I...see not as man sees...outward appearance ... I look at the heart" (16:7).

3. _____ . "Seven...sons passed before Samuel...the Lord has not chosen them (16:10).

4. David _____ . "He is keeping the sheep" (16:11).

5. David faithful in music skills. Recommended to king because he was "a skillful player of the harp" (16:16), and "can play well" (v. 17).

6. Refreshed the king. "David...played it (harp)...refreshed and well" (v. 21).

7. Daivd faithful to his sheep. "A lion, and a bear...took a lamb ... I went after it...caught it by its beard...killed it" (17:34-35).

B. DAVID—THE LORD HIS EXAMPLE/GOAL IN LIFE: PSALM 23

1. David wrote as a young sphered, "The Lord is my Shepherd" (v. 1):

   d. Primary protector.

   e. _____ .

   f. _____ .

2. The Lord was David's _____ :

   a. "I shall not want."

   b. "Lied...green pastures."

   c. "Still waters."

   d. "A table of food."

   e. "Full cup."

3. The Lord _____ Daivd. "Lead me in right paths" (v. 3).

4. _____ in danger. "Walk thought the valley of the shadow of death" (v. 4). Three comforting ideas:

   a. _____ .

   b. _____ .

   c. _____ .

5. To keep Daivd on course (v. 4):

    a. Rod – _____ .

    b. Staff – to _____ .

6. Three sources of strength (v. 5):

    a. _____ of food.

    b. Anoint head.

    c. Cup _____ .

7. Two watch dogs to watch over sheep and David (v. 6).

    a. Goodness of God to _____ .

    b. Mercy, to _____ .

8. Three conclusions:

    a. Because the Lord was David's Shepherd,
       _____ (v. 1).

    b. Because the Lord was with him,
       _____ (v. 4).

    c. Because of the Lord's loving kindness,
       _____ (v. 6).

C. TEN WAYS TO PREPARE TO BE GOD'S LEADER

1. _____ the work/ministry God has given you.

2. _____ so the work/ministry becomes you, and you are it.

3. _____ locate yourself with your work/ministry.

4. _____ yourself with your work/ministry, i.e., Daivd as shepherd.

5. _____ what God has given you.

6. _____ with the successes/failures of your work/ministry.

7. _____ faithfully your work/ministry.

8. _____ with the success/failures, and reward/loss of work/ministry.

9. _____ work/ministry totally.

10. _____ the rewards of work/ministry, i.e., meals, anoint head, God's house.

Lesson 2:

DAVID—FAITHFULLY FIGHTS EVIL

A. DAVID WAS NOT OLD ENOUGH

1. Nine foot Goliath **challenged** the army of Israel to send warriors to fight them. "If I prevail...you shall be our servants" (1 Samuel 17:9). "All the men of Israel...fled from him...dreadfully afraid" (17:24).

2. When David **volunteered**, "Eliab, his oldest brother...anger... pride" (17:28).

3. Argument against David, "You are a youth" (17:33).

4. Gave David Saul's **armor**. "Saul clothed David with his armor... helmet...coat of mail...David fastened his sword...tried to walk" (17:38-39).

5. There was a problem with **implied solution**. "I have not tested them" (17:39). So he took them off" (17:39).

B. DAVID'S PREPARATION TO FIGHT

1. **Tried and proven** weapons. "He took his staff...chose five smooth stones...and his sling" (17:40).

2. The **enemy**, Goliath began drawing near...the man who bore his shield went before him" (17:41).

3. Goliath's **challenge**. "Cursed David...I will give your flesh to the birds" (17:43-44).

4. David's **defense**. "You come...sword...spear...I come...in the name of the LORD of Host, the God of the armies of Israel" (17:45).

5. David's **prayer**. "The LORD does not save with sword...the battle is the Lord's...He will give you into our hands" (17:47).

6. **Tools** of God's victory. "David ran...took a stone...slung it...struck the Philistine in the forehead...sank in ... fell to his face" (17:49).

7. **Complete** the victory. "David ran...took his sword...cut off his head." "The Philistines saw ... and fled" (17:51). "David took the head...to Jerusalem ... put his (Goliath's) armor in his tent" (17:54).

8. Saul got **jealous**. "The women...came out to meet (King Saul) with singing and dancing...Saul has slain his thousands, David his ten thousands" (18:6). "Saul eyed David from that day" (18:9).

C. TEN STEPS TO FIGHT EVIL (ONE)

1. <u>Claim</u> the tools of faith used to win earlier/smaller victories (1 Samuel 17:34-36).

2. <u>Know</u> the source of your attack. "He has defiled the armies of the living God" (17:36).

3. Depend on <u>spiritual weapons</u> not secular weapons (17:23-24).

4. Be <u>aggressive</u>. "David hurried...toward...the Philistine" (17:48).

5. Use weapons that have given <u>victory in the past</u> (17:40).

6. <u>Faith</u> is your assurance. "I come to you in the name of the LORD of Host, the God of Israel" (17:45).

7. Remember your <u>testimony</u>. "That all the earth my know there is a God in Israel...this assembly shall know that the LORD...saves" (17:46-47).

8. Be <u>resolute</u>. "David slung...struck...the stone sank in...he fell... David ran and stood over...cut off his head" (17:49-51).

9. <u>Encourage</u> other. "The men of Israel...shouted...pursed the Philistines" (17:52).

10. <u>Document</u> your victory. "David took the head...brought it to Jerusalem" (17:54). "David before Saul, the head...in his hand" (17:57).

Lesson 2:

QUESTIONS

DAVID—FAITHFULLY FIGHTS EVIL

A. DAVID WAS NOT OLD ENOUGH

1. Nine foot Goliath _____ the army of Israel to send warriors to fight them. "If I prevail...you shall be our servants" (1 Samuel 17:9). "All the men of Israel...fled from him...dreadfully afraid" (17:24).

2. When David _____ , "Eliab, his oldest brother... anger...pride" (17:28).

3. Argument against David, "You are a youth" (17:33).

4. Gave David Saul's _____ . "Saul clothed David with his armor...helmet...coat of mail...David fastened his sword... tried to walk" (17:38-39).

5. There was a problem with _____ . "I have not tested them" (17:39). So he took them off" (17:39).

B. DAVID'S PREPARATION TO FIGHT

1. _____ weapons. "He took his staff...chose five smooth stones...and his sling" (17:40).

2. The _____ , Goliath began drawing near...the man who bore his shield went before him" (17:41).

3. Goliath's _____ . "Cursed David...I will give your flesh to the birds" (17:43-44).

4. David's _____ . "You come...sword...spear...I come...in the name of the LORD of Host, the God of the armies of Israel" (17:45).

5. David's _____ . "The LORD does not save with sword...the battle is the Lord's...He will give you into our hands" (17:47).

6. _____ of God's victory. "David ran...took a stone... slung it...struck the Philistine in the forehead...sank in ... fell to his face" (17:49).

7. _____ the victory. "David ran...took his sword... cut off his head." "The Philistines saw ... and fled" (17:51). "David took the head...to Jerusalem ... put his (Goliath's) armor in his tent" (17:54).

8. Saul got _____ . "The women...came out to meet (King Saul) with singing and dancing...Saul has slain his thousands, David his ten thousands" (18:6). "Saul eyed David from that day" (18:9).

C. TEN STEPS TO FIGHT EVIL (ONE)

1. _____ the tools of faith used to win earlier/smaller victories (1 Samuel 17:34-36).

2. _____ the source of your attack. "He has defiled the armies of the living God" (17:36).

3. Depend on _____ not secular weapons (17:23-24).

4. Be _____ . "David hurried...toward...the Philistine" (17:48).

5. Use weapons that have given _____ (17:40).

6. _____ is your assurance. "I come to you in the name of the LORD of Host, the God of Israel" (17:45).

7. Remember your _____ . "That all the earth my know there is a God in Israel...this assembly shall know that the LORD...saves" (17:46-47).

8. Be _____ . "David slung...struck...the stone sank in...he fell...David ran and stood over...cut off his head" (17:49-51).

9. _____ other. "The men of Israel...shouted...pursed the Philistines" (17:52).

10. _____ your victory. "David took the head... brought it to Jerusalem" (17:54). "David before Saul, the head...in his hand" (17:57).

Lesson 3:

DAVID—FAITHFULLY WRITING PSALMS TO GOD

A. DAVID LEARNING THE PSALMS

1. How did young David learn the Scriptures? **Applied Joshua**. "This book of the law shall not depart out of thy mouth...mediate... observe to do all that is written" (Joshua 1:8, NKJV).

2. Could David write? Reading and writing **required** of kings. "He shall write for himself a copy of this law (Deuteronomy) in a book...he shall read it all the days of his life" (Deuteronomy 17:18-19, NKJV).

3. David wrote 73 Psalms. Hebrew poetry is not rhyming the sounds of words, but repeats or restates the idea or thought. This amplified or drives home the meaning or message of the verse. "The Lord is my light and my salvation, whom shall I fear, the Lord is the strength of my life, of whom shall I be afraid" (Psalm 27:1).

4. When two lines expressing the opposite is called **antithetic parallelism**. "The LORD knoweth the way of the righteous; but the way of the ungodly shall perish" (Psalm 1:5).

5. David learned the faithfulness of God:

    a. **Parental** example/teaching.

    b. **Mediation** (Joshua 1:7-9).

    c. From sheep and nature.

B. KINDS OF PSALMS

1. Psalms of **lament**, tells God of a troubled situation. "Help, LORD for the godly man ceases! For the faithful disappear..." (Psalm 12:1). "If the foundation are destroyed, what can the righteous do?" (Psalm 11:3).

2. Psalms of **praise**. "O LORD, our LORD, how excellent is Your name in all the earth" (Psalm 8:1, 9).

3. Psalms of **thanksgiving**. "Sing praise to the Lord, you saints of His, give thanks at the remembrance of His name" (Psalm 30:4).

4. Psalms to **celebrate** God. "The heavens declare the glory of God, the firmament shows His handiwork" (Psalm 19:1).

5. Psalms of **wisdom**. "Delight yourself also in the Lord, and He shall give you the desires of your heart" (Psalm 37:4). "For evildoers shall be cut off; but those who wait on the Lord, they shall inherit the earth" (Psalm 37:9).

6. Psalms of **confidence**. "He leads me in the right paths according to His name when I walk through the valley of the shadows of death, I will fear no evil" (Psalm 23:3-4).

7. <u>Royal</u> Psalms. These show David as king and is a blessing to all the people. Some royal Psalms are prayers, thanksgivings, or predictions of Messiah (heir of David), focusing on the future. "He who sits in the heaven will laugh" (Psalm 2:4 ff).

8. Imprecatory Psalm. Where David prays for **judgment** on enemies. "Pour out Your indignation upon them, and let Your wrathful anger take hold of them. Let their dwelling place be desolate; let no one live in their tents" (Psalm 69:24-25).

C. TEN WAYS TO FIND GOD'S PRESENCE

1. Read Psalms to cultivate a **hunger** for God. "One thing I have desired of the Lord, that will I seek: that I may dwell in the house of the Lord all the days of my life, to behold the beauty of the Lord, and to inquire in His temple. For in the time of trouble He shall hide me in His pavilion; in the secret place of His tabernacle He shall hide me; He shall set me high upon a rock" (Psalm 27:4-5).

2. **Pray** the Psalms. Remember, "In the night, His song shall be with you" (Psalm 42:8, NLT). "May the words of my mouth and the meditation of my heart be pleasing to you, O Lord, my rock and my redeemer" (Psalm 19:4).

3. Write the Psalm out to **fully understand**. "My son, do not forget My law, but let your heart keep My commands for length of days and long life...bind them around your neck, write them on the tables of your heart" (Proverbs 3:1-3, NKJV).

4. Claim a **promise**. "when you are lonely or have deep needs. "I shall not want" (Psalm 23:1). When threatened physically. "I will fear no evil" (Psalm 23:4). When you doubt the future. "I will dwell in the house of the Lord forever" (Psalm 23:6).

5. Use Psalm to **worship** God. When David escaped Saul he wrote Psalm 18. "Therefore I will give thanks to You, O Lord, among the Gentiles, and sing praises to Your name" (Psalm 18:49).

6. Apply to your life the weight of <u>sin expressed</u> in a Psalm. "Have mercy upon me, O God, according to Your lovingkindness; according to the multitude of Your tender mercies, blot out my transgressions. For I acknowledge my transgressions, and my sin is always before me. Against You, You only, have I sinned, and done this evil in Your sight—that You may be found just when You speak, and blameless when You judge" (Psalm 51:1, 3-4).

7. <u>Realize</u> you are wonderfully and fearfully made. "O Lord, You have searched me and known me. I will praise You, for I am fearfully and wonderfully made; marvelous are Your works, and that my soul knows very well" (Psalm 139:1, 14).

8. When overwhelmed-stand bold to **thank** God. "He delivers me from my enemies. You also lift me up above those who rise against me; You have delivered me from the violent man. Therefore I will give thanks to You, O Lord, among the Gentiles, and sing praises to Your name" (Psalm 18:48-49).

9. Look at your **deep feelings** through the Psalm. "As the deer pants for the water brooks, so pants my soul for You, O God. Why are you cast down, O my soul? And why are you disquieted within me? Hope in God; for I shall yet praise Him, the help of my countenance and my God" (Psalm 42:1, 11).

10. **Memorize and mediate** the Psalms. "Your word I have hidden in my heart, that I might not sin against You" (Psalm 119:11).

Lesson 3:

QUESTIONS

DAVID—FAITHFULLY WRITING PSALMS TO GOD

A. DAVID LEARNING THE PSALMS

1. How did young David learn the Scriptures? _____ .
    "This book of the law shall not depart out of thy mouth...
    mediate...observe to do all that is written" (Joshua 1:8, NKJV).

2. Could David write? Reading and writing _____ of
    kings. "He shall write for himself a copy of this law (Deuteronomy)
    in a book...he shall read it all the days of his life" (Deuteronomy
    17:18-19, NKJV).

3. David wrote 73 Psalms. Hebrew poetry is not rhyming the sounds
    of words, but repeats or restates the idea or thought. This amplified
    or drives home the meaning or message of the verse. "The Lord
    is my light and my salvation, whom shall I fear, the Lord is the
    strength of my life, of whom shall I be afraid" (Psalm 27:1).

4. When two lines expressing the opposite is called _____ .
    "The LORD knoweth the way of the righteous; but the way of the
    ungodly shall perish" (Psalm 1:5).

5. David learned the faithfulness of God:

   a. _____ example/teaching.

   b. _____ (Joshua 1:7-9).

   c. From sheep and nature.

B. KINDS OF PSALMS

1. Psalms of _____ , tells God of a troubled situation. "Help, LORD for the godly man ceases! For the faithful disappear..." (Psalm 12:1). "If the foundation are destroyed, what can the righteous do?" (Psalm 11:3).

2. Psalms of _____ . "O LORD, our LORD, how excellent is Your name in all the earth" (Psalm 8:1, 9).

3. Psalms of _____ . "Sing praise to the Lord, you saints of His, give thanks at the remembrance of His name" (Psalm 30:4).

4. Psalms to _____ God. "The heavens declare the glory of God, the firmament shows His handiwork" (Psalm 19:1).

5. Psalms of _____ . "Delight yourself also in the Lord, and He shall give you the desires of your heart" (Psalm 37:4). "For evildoers shall be cut off; but those who wait on the Lord, they shall inherit the earth" (Psalm 37:9).

6. Psalms of _____ . "He leads me in the right paths according to His name when I walk through the valley of the shadows of death, I will fear no evil" (Psalm 23:3-4).

7. _____ Psalms. These show David as king and is a blessing to all the people. Some royal Psalms are prayers, thanksgivings, or predictions of Messiah (heir of David), focusing on the future. "He who sits in the heaven will laugh" (Psalm 2:4 ff).

8. Imprecatory Psalm. Where David prays for _____ on enemies. "Pour out Your indignation upon them, and let Your wrathful anger take hold of them. Let their dwelling place be desolate; let no one live in their tents" (Psalm 69:24-25).

C. TEN WAYS TO FIND GOD'S PRESENCE

1. Read Psalms to cultivate a _____ for God. "One thing I have desired of the Lord, that will I seek: that I may dwell in the house of the Lord all the days of my life, to behold the beauty of the Lord, and to inquire in His temple. For in the time of trouble He shall hide me in His pavilion; in the secret place of His tabernacle He shall hide me; He shall set me high upon a rock" (Psalm 27:4-5).

2. _____ the Psalms. Remember, "In the night, His song shall be with you" (Psalm 42:8, NLT). "May the words of my mouth and the meditation of my heart be pleasing to you, O Lord, my rock and my redeemer" (Psalm 19:4).

3. Write the Psalm out to _____ . "My son, do not forget My law, but let your heart keep My commands for length of days and long life...bind them around your neck, write them on the tables of your heart" (Proverbs 3:1-3, NKJV).

4. Claim a _____ . "when you are lonely or have deep needs. "I shall not want" (Psalm 23:1). When threatened physically. "I will fear no evil" (Psalm 23:4). When you doubt the future. "I will dwell in the house of the Lord forever" (Psalm 23:6).

5. Use Psalm to _____ God. When David escaped Saul he wrote Psalm 18. "Therefore I will give thanks to You, O Lord, among the Gentiles, and sing praises to Your name" (Psalm 18:49).

6. Apply to your life the weight of _____ in a Psalm. "Have mercy upon me, O God, according to Your lovingkindness; according to the multitude of Your tender mercies, blot out my transgressions. For I acknowledge my transgressions, and my sin is always before me. Against You, You only, have I sinned, and done this evil in Your sight—that You may be found just when You speak, and blameless when You judge" (Psalm 51:1, 3-4).

7. _____ you are wonderfully and fearfully made. "O Lord, You have searched me and known me. I will praise You, for I am fearfully and wonderfully made; marvelous are Your works, and that my soul knows very well" (Psalm 139:1, 14).

8. When overwhelmed-stand bold to _____ God. "He delivers me from my enemies. You also lift me up above those who rise against me; You have delivered me from the violent man. Therefore I will give thanks to You, O Lord, among the Gentiles, and sing praises to Your name" (Psalm 18:48-49).

9. Look at your _____ through the Psalm. "As the deer pants for the water brooks, so pants my soul for You, O God. Why are you cast down, O my soul? And why are you disquieted within me? Hope in God; for I shall yet praise Him, the help of my countenance and my God" (Psalm 42:1, 11).

10. _____ the Psalms. "Your word I have hidden in my heart, that I might not sin against You" (Psalm 119:11).

Lesson 4:

DAVID—FAITHFUL TO GOD'S CALLING

A. INTRODUCTION

1. Saul led 3,000 men against David (1 Samuel 24:2; 26:2).

2. David a man after God's heart, did not <u>sin against God</u>. David had two opportunities to kill Saul but followed God's highest calling. "En Gedi cave and Hachilah. "I would not stretch out my hand against the LORD'S anointed" (1 Samuel 26:23, NKJV).

3. Both occasions Saul led <u>**3,000 men**</u> (1 Samuel 24:2; 26:2).

B. EN GEDI, A CAVE WHERE DAVID AND MEN WERE HIDING: 1 SAMUEL 24:1-22

1. Saul came into a cave where David and his men were <u>**hiding**</u>. "David cut off a corner of Saul's robe" (24:4).

2. Followers tried to get David to <u>**kill Saul**</u>. "This is the day...the Lord delivered your enemy into your hands" (v. 4).

3. David pleaded **God's cause**. "The Lord forbid that I should do this thing to my master, the Lord's anointed, to stretch out my hand against him" (v. 6).

4. David called out to Saul. "See the corner of your robe in my hand" (v. 11). "I have not sinned against you"(v. 11).

5. Saul's **insincere apology**. "You are more righteous than I" (v. 17).

6. Saul's **prediction**. "I know you surely will be king" (v. 20).

C. HACHILAH—OPEN DESERT: 1 SAMUEL 26:1-15

1. Saul and 3,000 men **asleep**. "A deep sleep from the Lord had fallen on them" (v. 12).

2. David and Abishai **sneaked** into Saul's camp. "Saul lay sleeping... spear stuck into the ground" (v. 7).

3. **Revenge**. "Abishai...God has delivered your enemy into your hands...let me strike him" (v. 8).

4. **Commitment to God**. "The Lord forbid that I should stretch out my hand against the Lord's anointed" (v. 11).

5. Saul **recognized**. "Is that your voice, my son, David" (v. 17).

6. David's response. "Here is the king's spear" (v. 22).

7. Saul's **prediction**. "You shall do great things and also prevail" (v. 25).

D. TEN WAYS TO BE FAITHFUL
TO GOD'S GOALS FOR YOUR LIFE

1. It is never right, to do **wrong**, in the right way.

2. It is important to have **witnesses** to the good things you do.

3. Always remember **God's promises**. "Samuel took ... oil and anointed him" (1 Samuel 16:13).

4. Follow God's **providential** open doors/situations. Saul came into David's cave at En Gedi, but David went to Saul in the desert.

5. Don't be swayed by **bad advice** from good people.

6. Always be **guided** by what you know is right.

7. Don't **retaliate**, remember Saul had hurled the spear at David. "Saul sought to pin David to the wall with his spear" (1 Samuel 19:10). David returned the spear.

8. **Evidence** is one of your best arguments, i.e., corner of robe and spear.

9. Keep **safe distances**. "David came out of the cave" (24:8). "David went over to the other side" (26:13).

10. Accept others apologizes, but **be careful**.

Lesson 4:

DAVID—FAITHFUL TO GOD'S CALLING

A. INTRODUCTION

1. Saul led 3,000 men against David (1 Samuel 24:2; 26:2).

2. David a man after God's heart, did not _____ .
   David had two opportunities to kill Saul but followed God's
   highest calling. "En Gedi cave and Hachilah. "I would not stretch
   out my hand against the LORD'S anointed" (1 Samuel 26:23,
   NKJV).

3. Both occasions Saul led _____ (1 Samuel 24:2;
   26:2).

B. EN GEDI, A CAVE WHERE DAVID AND MEN WERE HIDING: 1 SAMUEL 24:1-22

1. Saul came into a cave where David and his men were _____
   . "David cut off a corner of Saul's robe" (24:4).

2. Followers tried to get David to _____ . "This is the day...the Lord delivered your enemy into your hands" (v. 4).

3. David pleaded _____ . "The Lord forbid that I should do this thing to my master, the Lord's anointed, to stretch out my hand against him" (v. 6).

4. David called out to Saul. "See the corner of your robe in my hand" (v. 11). "I have not sinned against you"(v. 11).

5. Saul's _____ . "You are more righteous than I" (v. 17).

6. Saul's _____ . "I know you surely will be king" (v. 20).

C. HACHILAH—OPEN DESERT:
1 SAMUEL 26:1-15

1. Saul and 3,000 men _____ . "A deep sleep from the Lord had fallen on them" (v. 12).

2. David and Abishai _____ into Saul's camp. "Saul lay sleeping... spear stuck into the ground" (v. 7).

3. _____ . "Abishai...God has delivered your enemy into your hands...let me strike him" (v. 8).

4. _____ . "The Lord forbid that I should stretch out my hand against the Lord's anointed" (v. 11).

5. Saul _____ . "Is that your voice, my son, David" (v. 17).

6. David's response. "Here is the king's spear" (v. 22).

7. Saul's _____ . "You shall do great things and also prevail" (v. 25).

D. TEN WAYS TO BE FAITHFUL TO GOD'S GOALS FOR YOUR LIFE

1. It is never right, to do _____ , in the right way.

2. It is important to have _____ to the good things you do.

3. Always remember _____ . "Samuel took ... oil and anointed him" (1 Samuel 16:13).

4. Follow God's _____ open doors/situations. Saul came into David's cave at En Gedi, but David went to Saul in the desert.

5. Don't be swayed by _____ from good people.

6. Always be _____ by what you know is right.

7. Don't _____ , remember Saul had hurled the spear at David. "Saul sought to pin David to the wall with his spear" (1 Samuel 19:10). David returned the spear.

8.   _____ is one of your best arguments, i.e., corner of robe and spear.

9.   Keep _____ . "David came out of the cave" (24:8). "David went over to the other side" (26:13).

10. Accept others apologizes, but _____ .

Lesson 5:

DAVID—FAITHFUL AS A NEW KING

A. INTRODUCTION

1. God anointed David as a teenager to be the future king:

   a. Saul's **disobedience**. "The Lord was sorry He had ever made Saul king" (1 Samuel 15:35).

   b. **Directed** by God. "This is the one, anoint him" (1 Samuel 16:12).

   c. **Half of life waited**. Anointed at age 15, then, "David was thirty years old when he began to reign...he reigned over Judah seven years and six months...he reigned over all Israel and Judah for thirty-three years" (2 Samuel 5:4-5, NLT).

   d. His great Psalms revealed his early **character**.

2. Twice David refused to kill Saul. "The Lord forbid that I should stretch out my hand against the Lord's anointed" (1 Samuel 24:6; 26:11).

B. DAVID KING OVER ONE TRIBE

1. Sought God's **direction**. "David asked the Lord about becoming king, 'Should I move back'...'Yes,' the Lord replied" (2 Samuel 2:1).

2. David obeyed. "David and his wives...his men and families **all** moved" (2 Samuel 2:2).

3. Public recognized David as king. "Then the men of Judah... anointed him" (2:4).

4. The northern tribes continued in **rebellion**:

   a. Saul's son Ishbosheth became **king**.

   b. War. "Beginning of a long war between...loyal to Saul...loyal to David" (3:1).

   c. Ishbosheth **murdered** (4:5-12).

C. DAVID KING OVER ALL ISRAEL: 2 SAMUEL 5

1. Recognition of Hebrew **heritage**. "All the tribes...came to David... saying, 'we are your own flesh and blood'" (2 Samuel 5:1, NLT).

2. Recognition of David's loyalty and God's choice:

   a. "In times past...you were the one...you led Israel" (2 Samuel 5:2).

   b. "The Lord said, 'You shall shepherd My people...be ruler over Israel'" (v. 2).

c. They anointed David king over Israel" (v. 3).

3. David establishes new capital in Jerusalem:

   a. Jerusalem inhabitants **mocked David**. "Even the blind and the lame will keep you out ... cannot come in" (v. 6).

   b. Joab climbed up the well into the pool of Silom (1 Chronicles 11:4-9).

D. TEN WAYS TO ENTER A NEW POSITION

1. Know **God has chosen** and appointed you (1 Samuel 16:1-3).

2. Make sure **God is leading you**. "The Lord said...'I have rejected (Saul)...I have provided a king'" (1 Samuel 16:1).

3. Be careful not to **run ahead of God's timing**. "David came by night...Saul lay sleeping." "The Lord forbid that I should stretch out my hand" (1 Samuel 26:9-11).

4. **Seek** God's guidance to move into the office. "David inquired of the Lord, 'shall I go up'" (2 Samuel 2:1).

5. Get **support and approval** of followers. "David...two wives ... the men who were with him...with household" (2 Samuel 2:2-3).

6. **Pray** for those not chosen. David prayed about Saul and Jonathan (2 Samuel 1:17-27).

7. **Identify** with those you will lead. "We are your own flesh and blood" (5:1, NLT).

8. Find a **permanent home** for ministry. "David took the stronghold of Zion (Jerusalem)...dwelt in the stronghold" (2 Samuel 5:7, 9, NKJV).

9. Be ready to **defend**. "Philistines heard...David king...they mobilized" (2 Samuel 5:17).

10. Put God in the **center**. "They brought the Ark of the Lord out sat it...inside the special tent David prepared" (2 Samuel 6:17, NLT).

Lesson 5:

DAVID — FAITHFUL AS A NEW KING

A. INTRODUCTION

1. God anointed David as a teenager to be the future king:

   a. Saul's _____ . "The Lord was sorry He had ever made Saul king" (1 Samuel 15:35).

   b. _____ by God. "This is the one, anoint him" (1 Samuel 16:12).

   c. _____ . Anointed at age 15, then, "David was thirty years old when he began to reign...he reigned over Judah seven years and six months...he reigned over all Israel and Judah for thirty-three years" (2 Samuel 5:4-5, NLT).

   d. His great Psalms revealed his early _____ .

2. Twice David refused to kill Saul. "The Lord forbid that I should stretch out my hand against the Lord's anointed" (1 Samuel 24:6; 26:11).

B. DAVID KING OVER ONE TRIBE

1. Sought God's _____ . "David asked the Lord about becoming king, 'Should I move back'...'Yes,' the Lord replied" (2 Samuel 2:1).

2. David obeyed. "David and his wives...his men and families _____ moved"
   (2 Samuel 2:2).

3. Public recognized David as king. "Then the men of Judah... anointed him" (2:4).

4. The northern tribes continued in _____ :

   a. Saul's son Ishbosheth became _____ .

   b. War. "Beginning of a long war between...loyal to Saul...loyal to David" (3:1).

   c. Ishbosheth _____ (4:5-12).

C. DAVID KING OVER ALL ISRAEL:
2 SAMUEL 5

1. Recognition of Hebrew _____ . "All the tribes... came to David...saying, 'we are your own flesh and blood'" (2 Samuel 5:1, NLT).

2. Recognition of David's loyalty and God's choice:

a. "In times past...you were the one...you led Israel" (2 Samuel 5:2).

b. "The Lord said, 'You shall shepherd My people...be ruler over Israel'" (v. 2).

c. They anointed David king over Israel" (v. 3).

3. David establishes new capital in Jerusalem:

a. Jerusalem inhabitants _____ . "Even the blind and the lame will keep you out ... cannot come in" (v. 6).

b. Joab climbed up the well into the pool of Silom (1 Chronicles 11:4-9).

D. TEN WAYS TO ENTER A NEW POSITION

1. Know _____ and appointed you (1 Samuel 16:1-3).

2. Make sure _____ . "The Lord said...'I have rejected (Saul)...I have provided a king'" (1 Samuel 16:1).

3. Be careful not to _____ . "David came by night... Saul lay sleeping." "The Lord forbid that I should stretch out my hand" (1 Samuel 26:9-11).

4. _____ God's guidance to move into the office. "David inquired of the Lord, 'shall I go up'" (2 Samuel 2:1).

5. Get _____ of followers. "David...two wives ... the men who were with him...with household" (2 Samuel 2:2-3).

6. _____ for those not chosen. David prayed about Saul and Jonathan (2 Samuel 1:17-27).

7. _____ with those you will lead. "We are your own flesh and blood" (5:1, NLT).

8. Find a _____ for ministry. "David took the stronghold of Zion (Jerusalem)...dwelt in the stronghold" (2 Samuel 5:7, 9, NKJV).

9. Be ready to _____ . "Philistines heard...David king...they mobilized" (2 Samuel 5:17).

10. Put God in the _____ . "They brought the Ark of the Lord out sat it...inside the special tent David prepared" (2 Samuel 6:17, NLT).

Lesson 6:

ANSWER KEY

DAVID—FAITHFUL TO REPENT AFTER TERRIBLE SIN

A. WHY DAVID GOT INTO ADULTERY: 2 SAMUEL 11

1. Didn't fulfill his job. "The times when Kings go to war...David sent Joab...remained at Jerusalem" (2 Samuel 11:1):

   a. **Getting older**.

   b. His past reputation would **help victory**.

   c. This battle was **smaller** than past.

2. **Sleeplessness**:

   a. Walk on roof.

   b. Bathsheba **bathing**.

   c. Beautiful to behold (v. 2).

   d. **Inquired**.

   e. Wife of Uriah (on battlefield).

f. Sent **messenger** (v. 4).

g. She came.

h. She lay with David.

i. "I am with child" (v. 5).

B. DAVID TRIED TO COVER UP:

1. Sent for Uriah, his "mighty men."

    a. Interviewed about war.

    b. **Sent home to wife**.

    c. Gave him food.

2. Uriah slept at David's quarters, "The Ark of God and the armies... open field...could I go home?" (v. 11).

3. David invited him to dinner...got him drunk...did not go home" (v. 13).

4. David's letter **carried by Uriah**. "Uriah on the front lines... fiercest...pull back...be killed" (v. 15).

5. David – adultery, lied, deceived, manslaughter, **involved others**.

C. DAVID'S SINS

1. **Marriage**. "Mourning was over...brought her to palace ... became one of his wives...the Lord was displease" (v. 26).

2. **God's message**. "Rich man...many sheep...poor man...one lamb... rich man killed it for his guest" (12:1-4).

3. Response. "David was furious" (v. 5). "He must pay fourfold" (v. 6).

   - **Death** of infant son

   - Rape of daughter Tamar

   - **Murder** of Amnon

   - Death of **Absalom**

D. DAVID'S REPENTANCE AND RESTORATION

1. **Seven day fast**. "David begged God to spare the child. He went without food and lay all night on the bare ground" (2 Samuel 12:16, NLT).

2. **David's determination**. "The elders of his household pleaded with him to get up and eat with them, but he refused" (v. 17).

3. Restoration. "He went to the Tabernacle and worshiped the Lord" (v. 20).

4. **Next King**. "David ... slept with her...gave birth to a son... Solomon" (v. 24).

E. TEN STEPS OF RESTORATION:
PSALM 51

1. Plead the **mercy of God**. "Have mercy upon me...according to Your multitude of mercies" (vv. 1-2).

2. Thoroughly confess your sins. "My iniquity...I acknowledge my transgressions" (vv. 2-3).

3. Realize sin is primarily against God, only secondarily against others and you. "**Against You**, You only have I sinned" (v. 4).

4. **Claim** God's judgment against sin. "That you may be just" (v. 4).

5. Ask for **cleansing**. "Purge me...I shall be clean, wash me...whitter than snow" (v. 7).

6. Remove sin completely. "Hide Your face from my sin" (v. 9).

7. **Worship**. "My tongue shall sing...my lips shall praise" (v. 14-15).

8. Ask for spirit filled **joy and power**. "Holy Spirit...joy of Your salvation" (v. 11-12).

9. **Service**. "I will teach transgressors Your ways" (v. 13).

10. **Enjoy restoration**. "You shall be please with sacrifices" (v. 19).

Lesson 6:

QUESTIONS

DAVID—FAITHFUL TO REPENT AFTER TERRIBLE SIN

A. WHY DAVID GOT INTO ADULTERY: 2 SAMUEL 11

1. Didn't fulfill his job. "The times when Kings go to war...David sent Joab...remained at Jerusalem" (2 Samuel 11:1):

   a. _____ .

   b. His past reputation would _____ .

   c. This battle was _____ than past.

2. _____ :

   a. Walk on roof.

   b. Bathsheba _____ .

   c. Beautiful to behold (v. 2).

   d. _____ .

   e. Wife of Uriah (on battlefield).

   f. Sent _____ (v. 4).

---

g. She came.

h. She lay with David.

i. "I am with child" (v. 5).

B. DAVID TRIED TO COVER UP:

1. Sent for Uriah, his "mighty men."

    a. Interviewed about war.

    b. _____ .

    c. Gave him food.

2. Uriah slept at David's quarters, "The Ark of God and the armies...
    open field...could I go home?" (v. 11).

3. David invited him to dinner...got him drunk...did not go home"
    (v. 13).

4. David's letter _____ . "Uriah on the front lines...
    fiercest...pull back...be killed" (v. 15).

5. David – adultery, lied, deceived, manslaughter, _____ .

C. DAVID'S SINS

1. _____ . "Mourning was over...brought her to
    palace ... became one of his wives...the Lord was displease" (v. 26).

2. _____ . "Rich man...many sheep...poor man...one lamb...rich man killed it for his guest" (12:1-4).

3. Response. "David was furious" (v. 5). "He must pay fourfold" (v. 6).

- _____ of infant son

- Rape of daughter Tamar

- _____ of Amnon

- Death of _____

D. DAVID'S REPENTANCE AND RESTORATION

1. _____ . "David begged God to spare the child. He went without food and lay all night on the bare ground" (2 Samuel 12:16, NLT).

2. _____ . "The elders of his household pleaded with him to get up and eat with them, but he refused" (v. 17).

3. Restoration. "He went to the Tabernacle and worshiped the Lord" (v. 20).

4. _____ . "David ... slept with her...gave birth to a son...Solomon" (v. 24).

E. TEN STEPS OF RESTORATION:
PSALM 51

1. Plead the _____ . "Have mercy upon me... according to Your multitude of mercies" (vv. 1-2).

2. Thoroughly confess your sins. "My iniquity...I acknowledge my transgressions" (vv. 2-3).

3. Realize sin is primarily against God, only secondarily against others and you. " _____ , You only have I sinned" (v. 4).

4. _____ God's judgment against sin. "That you may be just" (v. 4).

5. Ask for _____ . "Purge me...I shall be clean, wash me...whitter than snow" (v. 7).

6. Remove sin completely. "Hide Your face from my sin" (v. 9).

7. _____ . "My tongue shall sing...my lips shall praise" (v. 14-15).

8. Ask for spirit filled _____ . "Holy Spirit...joy of Your salvation" (v. 11-12).

9. _____ . "I will teach transgressors Your ways" (v. 13).

10. _____ . "You shall be please with sacrifices" (v. 19).

Lesson 7:

ANSWER KEY

DAVID—FAITHFUL AT THE END

A. GOD'S ETERNAL COVENANT WITH DAVID: 2 SAMUEL 7:1-29

1. Thinking of building a Temple (**house for God**). "David sat in his house...but the Ark of God dwells in tent curtains" (2 Samuel 7:1-2).

2. David's house will be **spiritual influence**. "When your days are finished...your seed after you...his kingdom forever" (vv. 12-13).

3. **Response**. "King David sat before the Lord, and said...the word which you have spoken...establish it forever" (v. 25).

B. PERMANENT LOCATION FOR TEMPLE: 2 SAMUEL 24:18-25

1. **Temple site**. "An altar on the threshing floor of Araunah" (v. 18).

2. **David bought**. "I will buy it...I will not offer burnt offerings to the Lord my God with that which cost me nothing" (v. 24).

C. PUT SOLOMON ON THE THRONE

1. David's son, "Adonijah exalted himself" (1 Kings 1:5). Gathered support...Joab...Abiathar the priest...had 50 men run before him... banquet to **announce he was king** (1 Kings 9:5-10).

2. David instructed Bathsheba, Nathan the prophet and Benaiah one of his mighty men, to do an **official inauguration**:

   a. Ride on my mule (1:37).

   b. Anoint at Gehon by Zadak the priest.

   c. Sit on my throne (v. 35).

   d. Blow horn to publicly announce (v. 34).

   e. Use official announcement, **long live King Solomon** (v. 34).

3. Told Adonijah at his banquet, "David has made Solomon king" (v. 43).

D. DAVID GATHERS BUILDING MATERIALS FOR TEMPLE

1. Not **built by David**. "The word of the Lord...you have shed much blood...made great wars ... you shall not build a house for My name" (1 Chronicles 22:8).

2. David **gathers supplies**. "40,000 tons of gold, 40,000 tons of silver, and so much iron and bronze that it cannot be weighed, timber and stones for the walls" (1 Chronicles 22:14, NLT).

3. David **gathers support**. "David ordered all the leaders...assist Solomon" (22:17).

4. **Vison casting**. "Build the sanctuary...bring the Ark of the Lord's Covenant...into the Temple" (22:19, NLT).

E. TEN WAYS TO EXTEND YOUR FAITHFULNESS AFTER YOU ARE GONE

1. **Plan** to put God at center of everything. David planned to honor the Lord's name" (1 Chronicles 22:19).

2. **Cast positive vision**. "The Temple...must be a magnificent structure, famous and glorious" (22:5).

3. Rally support **because of need**. "I am living in a beautiful palace, but the Ark of God is out there in a tent" (2 Samuel 7:2).

4. **Task** your loved ones to a great task. "David...instructed (Solomon) to honor the name of the LORD:

   a. God is with you (v. 11).

   b. Pray for wisdom, (v. 12).

   c. Remind to obey God (13).

   d. Do not be afraid or lose heart (v. 15).

5. Leave **directions and expectations**. Gave Solomon the plans. "David gave Solomon the plans – David gave instruction how much gold should be used...vast list of items (1 Chronicles 28:11-21).

6. Get **broad support**. "David summoned help from all the leaders.

7. Organize **support**. "David divided...into divisions" (23:6).

8. Explain **biblical** rational for task. "This is what the Lord declares...I have always...lived in a tent and a Tabernacle. as My dwelling place" (2 Samuel 7:5-6, NLT).

9. Pray for God's **continual blessing**. "Bless the house of your servant that I may continue" (2 Samuel 7:24).

10. Ask others to **follow your example**. "David challenged, 'Now then who will follow my example?'" (1 Chronicles 29:5, NLT).

Lesson 7:

QUESTIONS

DAVID — FAITHFUL AT THE END

A. GOD'S ETERNAL COVENANT WITH DAVID: 2 SAMUEL 7:1-29

1. Thinking of building a Temple (_____). "David sat in his house...but the Ark of God dwells in tent curtains" (2 Samuel 7:1-2).

2. David's house will be _____ . "When your days are finished...your seed after you...his kingdom forever" (vv. 12-13).

3. _____ . "King David sat before the Lord, and said... the word which you have spoken...establish it forever" (v. 25).

B. PERMANENT LOCATION FOR TEMPLE: 2 SAMUEL 24:18-25

1. _____ . "An altar on the threshing floor of Araunah" (v. 18).

2. _____ . "I will buy it...I will not offer burnt offerings to the Lord my God with that which cost me nothing" (v. 24).

C. PUT SOLOMON ON THE THRONE

1. David's son, "Adonijah exalted himself" (1 Kings 1:5). Gathered support...Joab...Abiathar the priest...had 50 men run before him... banquet to _____ (1 Kings 9:5-10).

2. David instructed Bathsheba, Nathan the prophet and Benaiah one of his mighty men, to do an _____ :

   a. Ride on my mule (1:37).

   b. Anoint at Gehon by Zadak the priest.

   c. Sit on my throne (v. 35).

   d. Blow horn to publicly announce (v. 34).

   e. Use official announcement, _____ (v. 34).

3. Told Adonijah at his banquet, "David has made Solomon king" (v. 43).

D. DAVID GATHERS
BUILDING MATERIALS FOR TEMPLE

1. Not _____ . "The word of the Lord...you have shed much blood...made great wars ... you shall not build a house for My name" (1 Chronicles 22:8).

2. David _____ . "40,000 tons of gold, 40,000 tons of silver, and so much iron and bronze that it cannot be weighed, timber and stones for the walls" (1 Chronicles 22:14, NLT).

3. David _____ . "David ordered all the leaders...assist Solomon" (22:17).

4. _____ . "Build the sanctuary...bring the Ark of the Lord's Covenant...into the Temple" (22:19, NLT).

E. TEN WAYS TO EXTEND YOUR
FAITHFULNESS AFTER YOU ARE GONE

1. _____ to put God at center of everything. David planned to honor the Lord's name" (1 Chronicles 22:19).

2. _____ . "The Temple...must be a magnificent structure, famous and glorious" (22:5).

3. Rally support _____ . "I am living in a beautiful palace, but the Ark of God is out there in a tent" (2 Samuel 7:2).

4. _____ your loved ones to a great task. "David... instructed (Solomon) to honor the name of the LORD:

a. God is with you (v. 11).

b. Pray for wisdom, (v. 12).

c. Remind to obey God (13).

d. Do not be afraid or lose heart (v. 15).

5. Leave _____ . Gave Solomon the plans. "David gave Solomon the plans – David gave instruction how much gold should be used...vast list of items (1 Chronicles 28:11-21).

6. Get _____ "David summoned help from all the leaders.

7. Organize _____ . "David divided...into divisions" (23:6).

8. Explain _____ rational for task. "This is what the Lord declares...I have always...lived in a tent and a Tabernacle. as My dwelling place" (2 Samuel 7:5-6, NLT).

9. Pray for God's _____ . "Bless the house of your servant that I may continue" (2 Samuel 7:24).

10. Ask others to _____ . "David challenged, 'Now then who will follow my example?'" (1 Chronicles 29:5, NLT).

PART FOUR

GOD SEEKER

POWERPOINT GUIDE

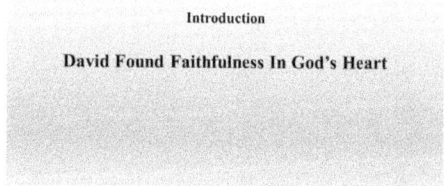

Introduction

David Found Faithfulness In God's Heart

INTRODUCTION

1. David the eighth son of Jesse (1 Samuel 16:10-11). Eight – new beginnings.

2. God rejected Saul. "The LORD said ... 'I have rejected him (Saul) ... fill your horn with oil ... go'" (1 Samuel 16:1).

3. Qualification: "The Lord seeth not as man seeth, man looketh on the outward appearance, but the Lord looketh on the heart" (1 Samuel 16:7, KJV). "God ... said, 'I have found David ... a man after My own heart'" (Acts 13:22).

CHAPTER 1

DAVID – FAITHFUL AS A YOUNG SHEPHERD

"I kept my father's sheep ... came a lion, and a bear, and took a lamb ... I went after ... I caught him by his beard and smote him" (1 Samuel 17:34-35). He learned, "The Lord is my Shepherd, I shall not want" (Psalm 23:1).

CHAPTER 2

DAVID – FAITHFULLY FOUGHT EVIL GOLIATH 1 SAMUEL 17:1-58

Not David's battle, but God was challenged. "Is there not a cause" (17:29). "He hast defied the armies of the Living God" (v. 36). "I come ... in the name of the LORD of Host ... whom thou has defied" (v. 45). "David prevailed over the Philstine with a sling and a stone" (v. 50).

CHAPTER 3

DAVID - FAITHFUL BY WRITING PSALMS TO GOD

David learn to read, write, and memorize Scriptures to fulfill the Old Testament command. "Observe to do according to all the law which Moses ... commanded you ... meditate on it day and night that you may observe it according to all that is written in it ... for the Lord your God is with you wherever you go" (Joshua 1:7-9).

CHAPTER 4

DAVID FAITHFUL TO GOD'S CALLING DIDN'T RUN AHEAD 1 SAMUEL 26:1-5

Saul chased David with 3,000 men to kill him (26:2). "David came by night ... Saul lay sleeping ... his spear stuck in the ground ... 'the Lord forbid that I should stretch out my hand against the Lord's anointed'" (26:9-11). "David took the spear ... cried to Abner ... you are worthy to die" (26:12-16).

CHAPTER 5

DAVID – FAITHFUL AS A NEW KING

"The Lord said to David ... 'go up to Hebron there they (Judah) anointed David king'" (2 Samuel 2:1-4). "Come all the tribes of Israel to David ... anointed David king" (2 Samuel 5:1-3). He made Jerusalem the capital and brought the Ark of the Covenant to the city.

CHAPTER 6

DAVID – FAITHFUL TO REPENT AFTER TERRIBLE SIN

"David sent Joab ... to battle ... David stayed in Jerusalem ... he saw a woman washing ... took her ... lay with her ... conceived ... 'I am with child'" (2 Samuel 11:1-5). David sent husband to her, he refused. Told Joab to put Uriah in fiercest battle and retreat. He was killed. David guilty. David married Bathsheba and child was born. Parable, "thou art the man" (12:7). Daivd fasted but the child died (Psalm 51).

Slide 9 of 82

CHAPTER 7

DAVID – FAITHFUL BEYOND HIS PHYSICAL LIFE

Bought threshing floor to build altar (future Temple site). "I will surely buy it ... offered burnt offering to the LORD" (2 Samuel 24:23). When Adonijah tried to make himself king, David from his sick bed, determined and planned Solomon's coronation.

Slide 10 of 82

Solomon ... shall reign after me" (1 Kings 1:30). God told Daivd, "Thou shalt not build me a house to dwell in" (1 Chronicles 17:4). Before his death, David prepared money, materials, stone, gold, silver, nails, and timber to build the Temple (1 Chronicles 22:14-19).

Slide 11 of 82

SEVEN LESSON IN COMING SERIES

1. Ten ways to prepare to be a faithful leader.
2. Ten steps to fight evil.
3. Ten ways to find God's presence.
4. How to fulfill life's calling.
5. How to enter a new position/job.
6. Ten steps to restoration.
7. Ten steps to extend your faithfulness after you are gone.

Slide 12 of 82

Lesson 1

David – Faithful As A Young Shepherd

Slide 13 of 82

A. DAVID – FIRST NOTICED: I SAMUEL 16:1

1. First noticed by God. "How long will you mourn for Saul ... I have provided Myself a king (among the sons of Jesse)" (1 Samuel 16:1).
2. Standard. "I ... see not as man sees ... outward appearance ... I look at the heart" (16:7).
3. Eighth chosen. "Seven ... sons passed before Samuel ... the Lord has not chosen them (16:10).

Slide 14 of 82

---

4. David faithful in daily task. "He is keeping the sheep" (16:11).
5. David faithful in music skills. Recommended to king because he was "a skillful player of the harp" (16:16), and "can play well" (v. 17).
6. Refreshed the king. "David ... played it (harp) ... refreshed and well" (v. 21).
7. Daivd faithful to his sheep. "A lion, and a bear ... took a lamb ... I went after it ... caught it by its beard ... killed it" (17:34-35).

Slide 15 of 82

B. DAVID – THE LORD HIS EXAMPLE/GOAL IN LIFE: PSALM 23

1. David wrote as a young sphered, "The Lord is my Shepherd" (v. 1):
   a. Primary protector.
   b. Personal.
   c. Present tense.

Slide 16 of 82

2. The Lord was David's provider:
   a. "I shall not want."
   b. "Lied ... green pastures."
   c. "Still waters."
   d. "A table of food."
   e. "Full cup."

3. The Lord guided Daivd.
   "Lead me in right paths" (v. 3).

Slide 17 of 82

4. Protected in danger. "Walk thought the valley of the shadow of death" (v. 4). Three comforting ideas:
   a. Through.
   b. Shadow.
   c. With me.

5. To keep Daivd on course (v. 4):
   a. Rod – correction.
   b. Staff – to protect or lift up.

Slide 18 of 82

6. Three sources of strength (v. 5):
   a. Table of food.
   b. Anoint head.
   c. Cup overflowing.

Slide 19 of 82

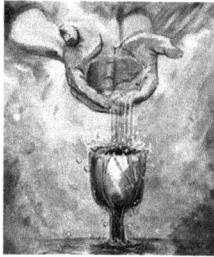

7. Two watch dogs to watch over sheep and David (v. 6).
   a. Goodness of God to overwhelm.
   b. Mercy, to forgive and restore.

Slide 20 of 82

8. Three conclusions:
   a. Because the Lord was David's Shepherd, I shall not want (v. 1).
   b. Because the Lord was with him, I will fear no evil (v. 4).
   c. Because of the Lord's loving kindness, I will dwell in the His house (v. 6).

Slide 21 of 82

C. TEN WAYS TO PREPARE TO BE GOD'S LEADER

1. Love the work/ministry God has given you.

2. Identify so the work/ministry becomes you, and you are it.

3. Presence locate yourself with your work/ministry.

4. Represent yourself with your work/ministry, i.e., Daivd as shepherd.

5. Protect what God has given you.

Slide 22 of 82

6. Feel with the successes/failures of your work/ministry.

7. Serve faithfully your work/ministry.

8. Associate with the success/failures, and reward/loss of work/ministry.

9. Support work/ministry totally.

10. Enjoy the rewards of work/ministry, i.e., meals, anoint head, God's house.

Slide 23 of 82

Lesson 2
David – Faithfully Fights Evil

Slide 24 of 82

A. DAVID WAS NOT OLD ENOUGH

1. Nine-foot Goliath challenged the army of Israel to send warriors to fight them. "If I prevail … you shall be our servants" (1 Samuel 17:9). "All the men of Israel … fled from him … dreadfully afraid" (17:24).
2. When David volunteered, "Eliab, his oldest brother … anger … pride" (17:28).
3. Argument against David, "You are a youth" (17:33).

Slide 25 of 82

4. Gave David Saul's armor. "Saul clothed David with his armor … helmet … coat of mail … David fastened his sword … tried to walk" (17:38-39).

5. There was a problem with implied solution. "I have not tested them" (17:39). So, he took them off" (17:39).

Slide 26 of 82

B. DAVID'S PREPARATION TO FIGHT

1. Tried and proven weapons. "He took his staff … chose five smooth stones … and his sling" (17:40).

2. The enemy, Goliath began drawing near … the man who bore his shield went before him" (17:41).

3. Goliath's challenge. "Cursed David … I will give your flesh to the birds" (17:43-44).

4. David's defense. "You come … sword … spear … I come … in the name of the LORD of Host, the God of the armies of Israel" (17:45).

Slide 27 of 82

5. David's prayer. "The LORD does not save with sword … the battle is the Lord's … He will give you into our hands" (17:47).

6. Tools of God's victory. "David ran … took a stone … slung it … struck the Philistine in the forehead … sank in … fell to his face" (17:49).

Slide 28 of 82

7. Complete the victory. "David ran … took his sword … cut off his head." "The Philistines saw … and fled" (17:51). "David took the head … to Jerusalem … put his (Goliath's) armor in his tent" (17:54).

Slide 29 of 82

8. Saul got jealous. "The women … came out to meet (King Saul) with singing and dancing … Saul has slain his thousands, David his ten thousands" (18:6). "Saul eyed David from that day" (18:9).

Slide 30 of 82

C. TEN STEPS TO FIGHT EVIL (ONE)

1. Claim the tools of faith used to win earlier/smaller victories (1 Samuel 17:34-36).

2. Know the source of your attack. "He has defiled the armies of the living God" (17:36).

3. Depend on spiritual weapons not secular weapons (17:23-24).

4. Be aggressive. "David hurried … toward … the Philistine" (17:48).

5. Use weapons that have given victory in the past (17:40).

Slide 31 of 82

6. Faith is your assurance. "I come to you in the name of the LORD of Host, the God of Israel" (17:45).

7. Remember your testimony. "That all the earth my know there is a God in Israel … this assembly shall know that the LORD … saves" (17:46-47).

8. Be resolute. "David slung … struck … the stone sank in … he fell … David ran and stood over … cut off his head" (17:49-51).

9. Encourage other. "The men of Israel … shouted … pursed the Philistines" (17:52).

10. Document your victory. "David took the head … brought it to Jerusalem" (17:54). "David before Saul, the head … in his hand" (17:57).

Slide 32 of 82

David –
Faithfully
Writing The
Psalms To God

Slide 33 of 82

A. DAVID LEARNING THE PSALMS

1. How did young David learn the Scriptures? Applied Joshua. "This book of the law shall not depart out of thy mouth … mediate … observe to do all that is written" (Joshua 1:8, NKJV).

2. Could David write? Reading and writing required of kings. "He shall write for himself a copy of this law (Deuteronomy) in a book … he shall read it all the days of his life" (Deuteronomy 17:18-19, NKJV).

Slide 34 of 82

3. David wrote 73 Psalms. Hebrew poetry is not rhyming the sounds of words but repeats or restates the idea or thought. This amplified or drives home the meaning or message of the verse. "The Lord is my light and my salvation, whom shall I fear, the Lord is the strength of my life, of whom shall I be afraid" (Psalm 27:1).

4. When two lines expressing the opposite is called antithetic parallelism. "The LORD knoweth the way of the righteous; but the way of the ungodly shall perish" (Psalm 1:5).

Slide 35 of 82

5. David learned the faithfulness of God:
   a. Parental example/teaching.
   b. Mediation (Joshua 1:7-9).
   c. From sheep and nature.

Slide 36 of 82

B. KINDS OF PSALMS

1. Psalms of lament, tells God of a troubled situation. "Help, LORD for the godly man ceases! For the faithful disappear…" (Psalm 12:1). "If the foundation are destroyed, what can the righteous do?" (Psalm 11:3).

2. Psalms of praise. "O LORD, our LORD, how excellent is Your name in all the earth" (Psalm 8:1, 9).

3. Psalms of thanksgiving. "Sing praise to the Lord, you saints of His, give thanks at the remembrance of His name" (Psalm 30:4).

Slide 37 of 82

4. Psalms to celebrate God. "The heavens declare the glory of God, the firmament shows His handiwork" (Psalm 19:1).

5. Psalms of wisdom. "Delight yourself also in the Lord, and He shall give you the desires of your heart" (Psalm 37:4). "For evildoers shall be cut off; but those who wait on the Lord, they shall inherit the earth" (Psalm 37:9).

6. Psalms of confidence. "He leads me in the right paths according to His name when I walk through the valley of the shadows of death, I will fear no evil" (Psalm 23:3-4).

Slide 38 of 82

7. Royal Psalms. These show David as king and is a blessing to all the people. Some royal Psalms are prayers, thanksgivings, or predictions of Messiah (heir of David), focusing on the future. "He who sits in the heaven will laugh" (Psalm 2:4 ff).

8. Imprecatory Psalm. Where David prays for judgment on enemies. "Pour out Your indignation upon them, and let Your wrathful anger take hold of them. Let their dwelling place be desolate; let no one live in their tents" (Psalm 69:24-25).

Slide 39 of 82

C. TEN WAYS TO FIND GOD'S PRESENCE

1. Read Psalm to cultivate a hunger for God. "One thing I have desired of the Lord, that will I seek: that I may dwell in the house of the Lord all the days of my life, to behold the beauty of the Lord, and to inquire in His temple. For in the time of trouble He shall hide me in His pavilion; in the secret place of His tabernacle, He shall hide me; He shall set me high upon a rock" (Psalm 27:4-5).

2. Pray the Psalms. Remember, "In the night, His song shall be with you" (Psalm 42:8, NLT). "May the words of my mouth and the meditation of my heart be pleasing to you, O Lord, my rock and my redeemer" (Psalm 19:4).

Slide 40 of 82

3. Write the Psalm out to fully understand. "My son, do not forget My law, but let your heart keep My commands for length of days and long life … bind them around your neck, write them on the tables of your heart" (Proverbs 3:1-3, NKJV).

4. Claim a promise. "when you are lonely or have deep needs. "I shall not want" (Psalm 23:1). When threatened physically. "I will fear no evil" (Psalm 23:4). When you doubt the future. "I will dwell in the house of the Lord forever" (Psalm 23:6).

Slide 41 of 82

5. Use Psalm to worship God. When David escaped Saul, he wrote Psalm 18. "Therefore, I will give thanks to You, O Lord, among the Gentiles, and sing praises to Your name" (Psalm 18:49).

6. Apply to your life the weight of sin expressed in a Psalm. "Have mercy upon me, O God, according to Your lovingkindness; according to the multitude of Your tender mercies, blot out my transgressions. For I acknowledge my transgressions, and my sin is always before me. Against You, You only, have I sinned, and done this evil in Your sight—that You may be found just when You speak, and blameless when You judge" (Psalm 51:1, 3-4).

Slide 42 of 82

7. Realize you are wonderfully and fearfully made. "O Lord, You have searched me and known me. I will praise You, for I am fearfully and wonderfully made; marvelous are Your works, and that my soul knows very well" (Psalm 139:1, 14).

8. When overwhelmed-stand bold to thank God. "He delivers me from my enemies. You also lift me up above those who rise against me; You have delivered me from the violent man. Therefore I will give thanks to You, O Lord, among the Gentiles, and sing praises to Your name" (Psalm 18:48-49).

Slide 43 of 82

9. Look at your deep feelings through the Psalm. "As the deer pants for the water brooks, so pants my soul for You, O God. Why are you cast down, O my soul? And why are you disquieted within me? Hope in God; for I shall yet praise Him, the help of my countenance and my God" (Psalm 42:1, 11).

10. Memorize and mediate the Psalms. "Your word I have hidden in my heart, that I might not sin against You" (Psalm 119:11).

Slide 44 of 82

Lesson 4

**David –
Faithful To
God's Calling**

Slide 45 of 82

A. INTRODUCTION

1. Saul led 3,000 men against David (1 Samuel 24:2; 26:2).

2. David a man after God's heart, did not sin against God. David had two opportunities to kill Saul but followed God's highest calling. "En Gedi cave and Hachilah. "I would not stretch out my hand against the LORD'S anointed" (1 Samuel 26:23, NKJV).

3. Both occasions Saul led 3,000 men (1 Samuel 24:2; 26:2).

Slide 46 of 82

B. BEN GEDI, A CAVE WHERE DAVID AND MEN WERE HIDING: 1 SAMUEL 24:1-22

1. Saul came into a cave where David and his men were hiding. "David cut off a corner of Saul's robe" (24:4).

2. Followers tried to get David to kill Saul. "This is the day … the Lord delivered your enemy into your hands" (v. 4).

3. David pleaded God's cause. "The Lord forbid that I should do this thing to my master, the Lord's anointed, to stretch out my hand against him" (v. 6).

Slide 47 of 82

4. David called out to Saul. "See the corner of your robe in my hand" (v. 11). "I have not sinned against you" (v. 11).

5. Saul's insincere apology. "You are more righteous than I" (v. 17).

6. Saul's prediction. "I know you surely will be king" (v. 20).

Slide 48 of 82

C. HACHILAH – OPEN DESERT: 1 SAMUEL 26:1-15

1. Saul and 3,000 men asleep. "A deep sleep from the Lord had fallen on them" (v. 12).

2. David and Abishai sneaked into Saul's camp. "Saul lay sleeping... spear stuck into the ground" (v. 7).

3. Revenge. "Abishai ... God has delivered your enemy into your hands ... let me strike him" (v. 8)

4. Commitment to God. "The Lord forbid that I should stretch out my hand against the Lord's anointed" (v. 11).

5. Saul recognized. "Is that your voice, my son, David" (v. 17).

6. David's response. "Here is the king's spear" (v. 22).

7. Saul's prediction. "You shall do great things and also prevail" (v. 25).

D. Ten Ways to Be Faithful To God's Goals For Your Life

1. It is never right, to do wrong, in the right way.

2. It is important to have witnesses to the good things you do.

3. Always remember God's promises. "Samuel took ... oil and anointed him" (1 Samuel 16:13).

4. Follow God's providential open doors/situations. Saul came into David's cave at En Gedi, but David went to Saul in the desert.

5. Don't be swayed by bad advice from good people.

6. Always be guided by what you know is right.

7. Don't retaliate, remember Saul had hurled the spear at David. "Saul sought to pin David to the wall with his spear" (1 Samuel 19:10). David returned the spear.

8. Evidence is one of your best arguments, i.e., corner of robe and spear.

9. Keep safe distances. "David came out of the cave" (24:8). "David went over to the other side" (26:13).

10. Accept others apologizes but be careful.

Lesson 5

David – Faithful As
A New King

A. INTRODUCTION

1. God anointed David as a teenager to be the future king:
   a. Saul's disobedience. "The Lord was sorry He had ever made Saul king" (1 Samuel 15:35).
   b. Directed by God. "This is the one, anoint him" (1 Samuel 16:12).
   c. Half of life waited. Anointed at age 15, then, "David was thirty years old when he began to reign ... he reigned over Judah seven years and six months ... he reigned over all Israel and Judah for thirty-three years" (2 Samuel 5:4-5, NLT).
   d. His great Psalms revealed his early character.

2. Twice David refused to kill Saul.

"The Lord forbid that I should stretch out my hand against the Lord's anointed" (1 Samuel 24:6; 26:11).

B. DAVID KING OVER ONE TRIBE

1. Sought God's direction. "David asked the Lord about becoming king, 'Should I move back' ... 'Yes,' the Lord replied" (2 Samuel 2:1).

2. David obeyed. "David and his wives ... his men and families all moved" (2 Samuel 2:2).

3. Public recognized David as king. "Then the men of Judah ... anointed him" (2:4).

4. The northern tribes continued in rebellion:
   a. Saul's son Ishbosheth became king.
   b. War. "Beginning of a long war between ... loyal to Saul ... loyal to David" (3:1).
   c. Ishbosheth murdered (4:5-12).

C. DAVID KING OVER ALL ISRAEL: 2 SAMUEL 5

1. Recognition of Hebrew heritage. "All the tribes ... came to David ... saying, 'we are your own flesh and blood'" (2 Samuel 5:1, NLT).

2. Recognition of David's loyalty and God's choice:
   a. "In times past ... you were the one ... you led Israel" (2 Samuel 5:2).
   b. "The Lord said, 'You shall shepherd My people ... be ruler over Israel'" (v. 2).
   c. They anointed David king over Israel" (v. 3).

3. David establishes new capital in Jerusalem:
   a. Jerusalem inhabitants mocked David. "Even the blind and the lame will keep you out ... cannot come in" (v. 6).
   b. Joab climbed up the well into the pool of Silom (1 Chronicles 11:4-9).

D. TEN WAYS TO ENTER A NEW POSITION

1. Know God has chosen and appointed you (1 Samuel 16:1-3).

2. Make sure God is leading you. "The Lord said ... 'I have rejected (Saul) ... I have provided a king'" (1 Samuel 16:1).

3. Be careful not to run ahead of God's timing. "David came by night ... Saul lay sleeping." "The Lord forbid that I should stretch out my hand" (1 Samuel 26:9-11).

4. Seek God's guidance to move into the office. "David inquired of the Lord, 'shall I go up'" (2 Samuel 2:1).

5. Get support and approval of followers. "David ... two wives ... the men who were with him ... with household" (2 Samuel 2:2-3).

6. Pray for those not chosen. David prayed about Saul and Jonathan (2 Samuel 1:17-27).

7. Identify with those you will lead. "We are your own flesh and blood" (5:1, NLT).

8. Find a permanent home for ministry. "David took the stronghold of Zion (Jerusalem) ... dwelt in the stronghold" (2 Samuel 5:7, 9, NKJV).

9. Be ready to defend. "Philistines heard ... David king ... they mobilized" (2 Samuel 5:17).

10. Put God in the center. "They brought the Ark of the Lord out sat it ... inside the special tent David prepared" (2 Samuel 6:17, NLT).

Lesson 6

David –
Faithful To Be
Restored After
Terrible Sin

A. WHY DAVID GOT INTO ADULTERY: 2 SAMUEL 11

1. Didn't fulfill his job. "The times when kings go to war ... David sent Joab ... remained at Jerusalem" (2 Samuel 11:1):
   a. Getting older.
   b. His past reputation would help victory.
   c. This battle was smaller than past.

2. Sleeplessness:
   a. Walk on roof.
   b. Bathsheba bathing.
   c. Beautiful to behold (v. 2).
   d. Inquired.
   e. Wife of Uriah (on battlefield).
   f. Sent messenger (v. 4).
   g. She came.
   h. She lay with David.
   i. "I am with child" (v. 5).

B. DAVID TRIED TO COVER UP:

1. Sent for Uriah, his "mighty men."
   a. Interviewed about war.
   b. Sent home to wife.
   c. Gave him food.

2. Uriah slept at David's quarters, "The Ark of God and the armies ... open field ... could I go home?" (v. 11).

3. David invited him to dinner ... got him drunk ... did not go home" (v. 13).

4. David's letter carried by Uriah. "Uriah on the front lines ... fiercest ... pull back ... be killed" (v. 15).

5. David – adultery, lied, deceived, manslaughter, involved others.

C. DAVID'S SINS

1. Marriage. "Mourning was over ... brought her to palace ... became one of his wives ... the Lord was displeased" (v. 26).

2. God's message. "Rich man ... many sheep ... poor man ... one lamb ... rich man killed it for his guest" (12:1-4).

3. Response. "David was furious" (v. 5). "He must pay fourfold" (v. 6).

- Death of infant son
- Rape of daughter Tamar
- Murder of Amnon
- Death of Absalom

D. DAVID'S REPENTANCE AND RESTORATION

1. Seven day fast. "David begged God to spare the child. He went without food and lay all night on the bare ground" (2 Samuel 12:16, NLT).

2. David's determination. "The elders of his household pleaded with him to get up and eat with them, but he refused" (v. 17).

3. Restoration. "He went to the Tabernacle and worshiped the Lord" (v. 20).

4. Next King. "David ... slept with her ... gave birth to a son ... Solomon" (v. 24).

E. TEN STEPS OF RESTORATION: PSALM 51

1. Plead the mercy of God. "Have mercy upon me ... according to Your multitude of mercies" (vv. 1-2).

2. Thoroughly confess your sins. "My iniquity ... I acknowledge my transgressions" (vv. 2-3).

3. Realize sin is primarily against God, only secondarily against others and you. "Against You, You only have I sinned" (v. 4).

4. Claim God's judgment against sin. "That you may be just" (v. 4).

5. Ask for cleansing. "Purge me ... I shall be clean, wash me ... whitter than snow" (v. 7).

6. Remove sin completely. "Hide Your face from my sin" (v. 9).

7. Worship. "My tongue shall sing ... my lips shall praise" (v. 14-15).

8. Ask for spirit filled joy and power. "Holy Spirit ... joy of Your salvation" (v. 11-12).

9. Service. "I will teach transgressors Your ways" (v. 13).

10. Enjoy restoration. "You shall be please with sacrifices" (v. 19).

Lesson 7

David –
Faithful
Beyond His
Physical Life

**A. GOD'S ETERNAL COVENANT WITH DAVID:
2 SAMUEL 7:1-29**

1. Thinking of building a Temple (house for God). "David sat in his house ... but the Ark of God dwells in tent curtains" (2 Samuel 7:1-2).

2. David's house will be spiritual influence. "When your days are finished ... your seed after you ... his kingdom forever" (vv. 12-13).

3. Response. "King David sat before the Lord, and said ... the word which you have spoken ... establish it forever" (v. 25).

**B. PERMANENT LOCATION FOR TEMPLE:
2 SAMUEL 24:18-25**

1. Temple site. "An altar on the threshing floor of Araunah" (v. 18).

2. David bought. "I will buy it ... I will not offer burnt offerings to the Lord my God with that which cost me nothing" (v. 24).

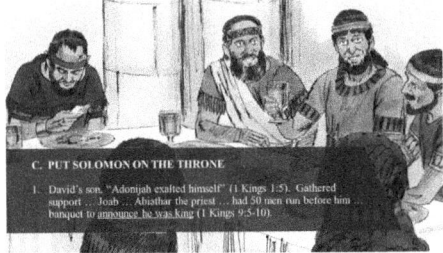

C. PUT SOLOMON ON THE THRONE

1. David's son. "Adonijah exalted himself" (1 Kings 1:5). Gathered support ... Joab ... Abiathar the priest ... had 50 men run before him banquet to announce he was king (1 Kings 9:5-10).

2. David instructed Bathsheba, Nathan the prophet and Benaiah one of his mighty men, to do an official inauguration:
   a. Ride on my mule (1:37).
   b. Anoint at Gehon by Zadak the priest.
   c. Sit on my throne (v. 35).
   d. Blow horn to publicly announce (v. 34).
   e. Use official announcement, long live King Solomon (v. 34).

3. Told Adonijah at his banquet. "David has made Solomon king" (v. 43).

D. DAVID GATHERS BUILDING MATERIALS FOR TEMPLE

1. Not built by David. "The word of the Lord ... you have shed much blood ... made great wars ... you shall not build a house for My name" (1 Chronicles 22:8).

2. David gathers supplies. "40,000 tons of gold, 40,000 tons of silver, and so much iron and bronze that it cannot be weighed, timber and stones for the walls" (1 Chronicles 22:14, NLT).

3. David gathers support. "David ordered all the leaders ... assist Solomon" (22:17).

4. Vision casting. "Build the sanctuary ... bring the Ark of the Lord's Covenant ... into the Temple" (22:19, NLT).

E. TEN WAYS TO EXTEND YOUR FAITHFULNESS AFTER YOU ARE GONE

1. Plan to put God at center of everything. David planned to honor the Lord's name" (1 Chronicles 22:19).

2. Cast positive vision. "The Temple ... must be a magnificent structure, famous and glorious" (22:5).

3. Rally support because of need. "I am living in a beautiful palace, but the Ark of God is out there in a tent" (2 Samuel 7:2).

4. Task your loved ones to a great task. "David … instructed (Solomon) to honor the name of the LORD:
   a. God is with you (v. 11).
   b. Pray for wisdom, (v. 12).
   c. Remind to obey God (13).
   d. Do not be afraid or lose heart (v. 15).

5. Leave directions and expectations. Gave Solomon the plans – David gave instruction how much gold should for future success. "David be used … vast list of items (1 Chronicles 28:11-21).

6. Get broad support. "David summoned help from all the leaders.

7. Organize support. "David divided … into divisions" (23:6).

8. Explain biblical rational for task. "This is what the Lord declares … I have always … lived in a tent and a Tabernacle. as My dwelling place" (2 Samuel 7:5-6, NLT).

9. Pray for God's continual blessing. "Bless the house of your servant that I may continue" (2 Samuel 7:24).

10. Ask others to follow your example. "David challenged, 'Now then who will follow my example?'" (1 Chronicles 29:5, NLT).

PART FIVE

GOD SEEKER

ADDITIONAL RESOURCES

POWERPOINT SLIDES:

To purchase and download the Powerpoint Slides go to
https://www.norimediagroup.com/pages/elmer-towns

VIDEO:

To purchase available video by Dr. Towns go to
https://www.norimediagroup.com/pages/elmer-towns

ADD-ON CONTENT

To purchase additional products in this series go to
https://www.norimediagroup.com/pages/elmer-towns

RELATED BOOKS

My Name is the Holy Spirit: Discover Me through My Name
Available at https://www.norimediagroup.com/pages/elmer-towns

From

ELMER L. TOWNS

The Ten
Most Influential
Churches
of the Past Century
HOW THEY IMPACT YOU TODAY

ELMER L. TOWNS
Bestselling Author of Fasting for Spiritual Breakthrough

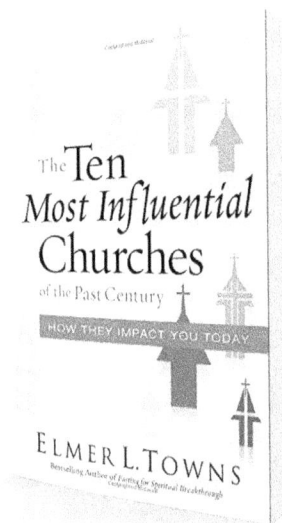

Your Church Can Influence the World

History has shown that great leaders have the ability to reach beyond the walls of their churches to influence cultures for Christ. We've seen it in the Pentecostal/Charismatic movement, in the explosive growth of house churches in Communist China, in the expansion of the Southern Baptist Convention, and in the world-wide rise of praise and worship music led by Hillsong Church, among other phenomena.

In *The Ten Most Influential Churches of the Past Century*, Dr. Elmer Towns presents evidence of the powerful influence of these churches and how their innovative strategies and faith accomplish these goals. Then he tells how you can apply these principles to your church. You will learn how some of the most influential leaders in Church history became conduits for your future ministry and how your church can experience exponential growth.

Most importantly, you will see that the great results in these ten churches grow out of the power of the Word of God, the ministry of many dedicated lay workers, the faith-producing ministry of great leaders—all under the anointing of the Holy Spirit.

Purchase your copy wherever books are sold

From

ELMER L. TOWNS

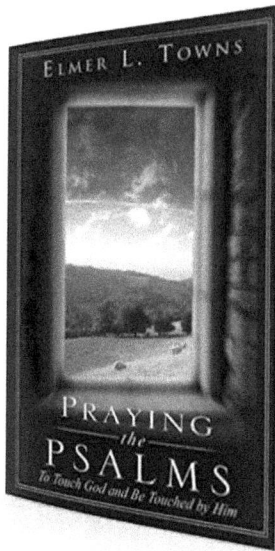

The Book of Psalms reflects the heart of God. *Praying the Psalms* carefully shapes the Psalms into personal prayers enabling you to identify with the Psalmist as he prayed. The author, Dr. Towns, is living breathing testimony of the power and fulfillment you will experience as you read the pages of this most powerful book.

The Psalmist poured our his soul to God concerning the things that deeply moved him. As you read the Psalms, you are taking a peak into his heart. You will weep when he weeps, should when he rejoices, burn when he gets angry and fall on your face when he worships God.

Purchase your copy wherever books are sold

From

ELMER L. TOWNS

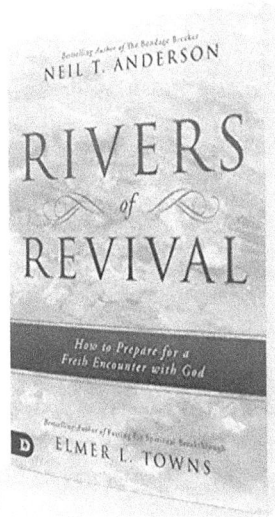

Since the Day of Pentecost, seasons of revival and awakening have brought refreshing to the spiritually dry, life to the spiritually dead, and miraculous encounters with the Holy Spirit.

In this timely and prophetic volume, two bestselling generals of the faith, Dr. Elmer Towns and Dr. Neil T. Anderson, offer collective wisdom, insight, and strategy on how you can experience and release a river of Holy Spirit outpouring into your world!

Additionally, Drs. Towns and Anderson have compiled contributions from other key authorities on revival who have encountered the move of God firsthand. Each contributor provides practical wisdom on how you can experience the Spirit's touch in your own life, church and even geographical region.

A fresh move of God is on the way. Prepare yourself to experience Holy Spirit outpouring like never before!

Purchase your copy wherever books are sold

From

ELMER L. TOWNS

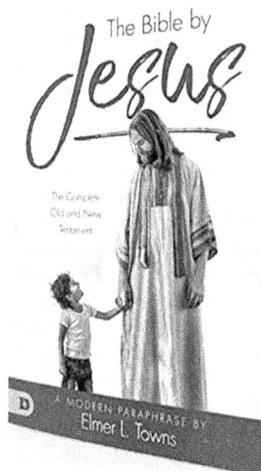

The Bible is the only answer that can satisfy the longing of every human heart

The Bible by Jesus is a unique presentation of the Scriptures from the perspective of Jesus the Author Himself. This powerful paraphrase of the Old and New Testaments will usher you into a fresh level of intimate experience with God through His Word.

You will see Christ in every book of the Bible. Then you will understand Scripture that transforms your life.

- Encounter the Old Testament as a gateway to know Jesus.
- Read to hear the voice of Jesus speaking through the Gospel as He tells you of His birth, ministry, death and resurrection.
- Experience Acts, the epistles, and the book of Revelation to know Jesus and His will for our life.

Read the pages of Scripture to hear the Son of God Himself and draw near to encounter His presence.

Purchase your copy wherever books are sold

www.ingramcontent.com/pod-product-compliance
Lightning Source LLC
Chambersburg PA
CBHW060005100426
42740CB00010B/1405

* 9 7 8 0 7 6 8 4 6 2 8 8 3 *